WHAT'S AGE GOT TO DO WITH IT?

WHAT'S AGE GOT TO DO WITH IT?

A Celebration of Life

Second Edition

Shirley Zarrilli

Changing Lifestyles in the New Millennium

KENDALL/HUNT PUBLISHING COMPANY
4050 Westmark Drive Dubuque, Iowa 52002

Library of Congress Catalog Card Number: 99-69741

ISBN 0-7872-6776-7

Printed in the United States of America
10 9 8 7 6 5 4 3 2 1

Dedication

I was inspired to write this book to reassure and to take the fear out of anyone approaching retirement. Day after day, I would talk to couples or single people getting ready to retire. They were always scared to death. The look on their faces were always the same. A tear was ready to fall if anyone said something about selling their home. I would ask them, "Is this the first time you ever visited an active adult community?"

This is for all you people thinking about retirement. Don't be afraid to visit an active adult community. Life is not over. Please believe me, the best is yet to come. You are approaching a new stage in your life. The best is coming, I know, it is a Celebration!!!

Dedicated to:

—My Mother—

Because through her enthusiasm, independence, energy, bubbly personality and the love of life, she gave me the same love of life.

Sincere Thanks to:

All My very cherished Active Adult friends, who I have met through the years. Who have inspired me to write this book. Love to all of You.

"It's a Celebration of Life"

ACKNOWLEDGMENTS

To My Sister Joyce:

For her love,
Who never stopped believing
in me and encouraged me
to complete my book.

To My Sister Lorraine and Brother Jack:

Who made our family a solid unit,
and who was always there for me.

To My Three Jewels:

Richard, Mark and Anthony
Thank you Sons for all the
joy and happiness you have given to me.

To My Husband Richard:

Who has been my Love
and Rock in Life.

To My Four Grandchildren:

Kaitlyn, nine years old,
Richard Jr., six years old,
Shannon, four years old,
and Hanna, nine months old,
will continue
the flow of love
in our family circle.

TABLE OF CONTENTS

TABLE OF CONTENTS

The most important thing I do in working with mature adults contemplating retirement is to convey to them just how positive retirement can be. Fortunately for me, that task is made easier by the fact that it is true and also by my own attitude—a gift that I received from my mother.

My mother has been a motivation and inspiration to me throughout my life. I have rarely met a person with a more positive attitude to life. She was only forty-two when my father died. Society being what it was then, she could have easily donned black for the rest of her life. However, my mother would never have given up her own life—or the lives of her children—so readily. She took charge of her life. She got a job and supported her family. More to the point, she supported herself. She took good care of herself, dressing well, remaining concerned about her body and her image.

She made a point of smiling every morning when she got up.

Even today, I am amazed at how wonderfully that simple " smile a day " works to make my life more enjoyable. It practically shouts to me—and everyone I meet—that my life is mine to enjoy as much as I can.

Take charge of your life! That's what happiness is all about and that's what retirement is all about too.

Most of the mature adults I've been working with for these past ten years have successfully raised their children and seen them move out of the house—and then found themselves with houses that had suddenly become too large and empty. These adults don't want to become couch potatoes, slaves to the daytime talk shows! The women don't want to end up spending their days in house dresses. The men don't want to " tinker." They want to do the things they enjoy, they challenge them.

The bad news is that too many people do end up becoming couch potatoes. Too many women watch daytime television for want of anything else to do. Too many men tinker because they are bored. The good news is that you don't have to! This is not the " fate that awaits you when you retire."

Every day I talk with people who believe that it's their time for some fun—but they're not sure how to have fun anymore. They know they're not satisfied but they don't know what to do about it.

These people—maybe you're included in this group—aren't comfortable making changes because they only seem to be able to think of what they'll be "leaving behind." I tell them that it's funny how fiercely we cling to things, even those things that make us unhappy, simply because we don't really understand what's out there.

There is so *much* out there! Welcome to the new millennium! People in their fifties and sixties and beyond are not leaving things behind so much as embracing all the possibilities ahead!

There are many active, healthy years ahead.

My message is simple. With all those wonderful years still to come isn't it about time to think about how you're going to spend them?

Step one is so wonderfully simple.
—Smile.

Step two" —Tell yourself you deserve all the fun you're going to have!

Chapter One
How to be Happy

I'd be a millionaire if I had a penny for every time someone said to me that they only wanted to be *happy*, that nothing else was so important as being happy and finding joy in life.

The problem is, happiness is a slippery thing and it means different things to different people. However, there are so many things that you can do to help yourself be happy—live in a place that is comfortable, be surrounded by people who are interesting and *interested*, be active!

"Oh, Shirley," one woman said to me one time, "I know I should be happy, but I don't even know if I am happy."

Her comment started me thinking. It was curious to me that someone might not even be sure whether or not they were happy. So, I decided to come up with a list of concrete ways you could know that you were happy.

When I finished my list, I returned to the woman who had made that curious comment to me and I shared my list with her. I hadn't gotten half-way through it before she was smiling and nodding her head.

"You're right, Shirley. Hit the nail right on the head."

The first item on my list is there only partially in jest—you know you're happy when your grandson asks you if he can borrow your BMW. Our society associates certain material possessions with young people, but there is no sane reason why older, active adults shouldn't enjoy the same things that younger people enjoy.

I think that it happens more often than those people on Madison Avenue realize.

The second item on my list is, You know you're happy when your neighbor asks you where you work out. "You look terrific!"

Study after study has shown that when we remain physically active and engaged, we are healthier and happier. The machinery of our lives—our bodies—need regular challenges, maintenance and activity to keep running smoothly. The "icing on the cake" is that physical activity also results in our looking healthy, looking good. And all of us want to look our best.

Happiness is when your son asks you what you made for dinner and your honest answer is, "Reservations." Sure, I know that this is the tag line for a joke, but I also know that too many of our sons and daughters expect us to live boring and staid little lives after retirement. I'm not entirely sure what they picture in their minds—a bowl of gruel by five-thirty and then an hour of television and then to bed?

We know that a happy life is an active life. That means getting out and *doing* things. There's nothing wrong in preparing a lovely meal. By the same token, there's nothing wrong in getting out and enjoying a lovely meal without the work involved in cooking or cleaning.

Happiness is... wearing bleached-out jeans! Oh, I know many of our fashion ideas do not lend themselves to blue jeans, but the important thing to remember is that when we reach our retirement years we do not don grays and blacks. We can—and should—remain stylish.

Youth—in the sense of exuberance and the pleasure we take in the world around us—is often reflected in how we present ourselves to the world. A strong, healthy body. Young fashions. Concern for our skin and hair. This is all what happiness is about as well.

Happiness is—impatience. Impatience? Well, not impatience itself, but impatience for the next social dance. *Wanting* to do things that are fun. Who among us doesn't enjoy being with other people, or more to the point, enjoy the sounds of good music while gliding across a dance floor?

"Okay, Shirley," my friend said, "I get the picture..."

"But there are so many more things on the list!" I said. "For example, you know you're happy when you're out playing tennis—before breakfast."

She chuckled at that.

"I'm serious," I told her. "Or how about, you laugh so hard your stomach hurts?"

She nodded her head. "That's a good one."

I explained that I had approached my list very seriously. Having heard people talk about "being happy" for so long, I really gave a lot of thought to specific things that would help people realize when they were happy.

Participating in five, ten and 20 kilometer cycling events.

"So much of your happiness list has to do with activity," my friend pointed out.

"Exactly! Happiness has a great deal to do with being and remaining active. But my list doesn't only include physical activities. For example, you know you're happy when the perfume you bought cost $80 an ounce."

Her eyes widened.

"Don't you see, we all deserve an extravagance now and again. For people in their retirement years, people who have most likely sacrificed many things for their children, for their homes—for their retirement years—small luxuries are our rewards."

"Of course, it doesn't have to be perfume. It can be a new dress. A new set of golf clubs. A vacation. Whatever. The point is, happiness is treating ourselves like we are the special people we are."

"Well," she said, "What else do you have on that list of yours?"

"How about making a date with your honey to see the latest movie in town?"

"That sounds good. I noticed you used the term 'honey' rather than..."

"Spouse?" Whether because of divorce or death, many people of retirement age are not married. But that doesn't mean that they shouldn't have a full and active social life. Being part of a community is a wonderful feeling, but having someone special really makes a difference in our lives.

"All of us deserve that."

That observation led to the next item on my list. Happiness is when you find that good-looking person on the other side of the bus is winking at you!

Happiness is recognizing that we are attractive. No, we don't have to be "bombshells" and "knock-outs"—except to our special someone.

Now, I had to admit that a couple of items on my list were somewhat silly. After all, how many of us have to beg off a dinner invitation from Donald Trump because we are too busy? Not many, right? But the essential truth is obvious. When you are active, you are happy. The more active you are, the happier you are.

Active and involved. The dynamic duo of happiness! Keeping abreast of what's happening in the world and being active in your life. Wouldn't it be better to have the *Wall Street Journal* delivered to your door rather than the doctors' bills?

You bet.

Of course, the final item on the list is probably the silliest. Happiness is buying yourself Nintendo for Christmas.

"Shirley, you are the best," my friend said. "I feel happier just hearing your list."

"The thing is, you should realize that you *can* be happy. Happiness isn't something available only to those saintly souls who climb mountain tops and meditate. Happiness is something that is accessible to all of us, everyday."

"You know, I was thinking. Your list could be renamed."

"Renamed? Really?"

"Sure. Instead of 'Happiness is...' it could have been named, 'Active Retired Adult Living is...'"

I thought about it for a second and realized that my friend was right. "I guess that I really believe that an active life in the retirement years is happiness," I concluded.

Active and involved. Not only the definition of happiness but the definition of the active, retired life as well.

Chapter Two
Looking Good!

Growing older today doesn't mean accruing years. What it really means is—Getting Better! Today men and women are staying younger longer in both body and mind.

Men and women take more classes, are involved in more study and interest groups than ever before. Their minds are remaining young and supple. And so are their bodies. Many are healthier during their retirement years than they ever were before.

The secret is really no secret at all. Keep active!

Keeping active contributes to a positive attitude. Once you have a positive attitude all things are possible. Think positive! Think young! There's no reason to fear something just because you haven't done it before. Go dancing. Go boating, biking, hiking.

I keep telling people that if they think young they'll stay young.

Taking care of your mind and your body is the important thing. For example, not too long ago I read a letter to Ann Landers. In it, a woman described herself as being "big boned." She wrote that she kept a refrigerator full or chocolate because she was a chocolate addict, but that in spite of it, she was determined to keep her weight down. She asked Ann if she thought it was folly for her to be so concerned with her weight. "I'm a widow and still socially active..." she noted. "But I'm also 83 years old. Should I spend my remaining years resisting chocolate, or should I just go on and be fat and sloppy?

Although chocolate was the immediate issue in the letter, the underlying question had to do with age. After all, a 21 year old would never ask whether she should just go on and be fat and sloppy for her remaining years.

The woman, "Chocolate Addict in El Paso," was certainly young at heart. Her dilemma was at the heart of her attitude toward life. At 83, she was still socially active, still concerned with how she looked; however, she felt that craving for chocolate all the time.

Ann Landers suggested a visit to a nutritionist so that she could , literally, have her cake and eat it too—in moderation. However, the sub text was also clear, you're never old enough to simply "let yourself go."

Feeling good has everything to do with looking good and looking good starts at the top of your head and goes down to the tips of your toes.

Ladies, get rid of the washed out gray! Color

your hair to accent your natural beauty. Pick a shade that's a bit lighter than when you were younger—this will brighten your face. You see, the goal is not vanity in the sense that you want to be young; rather, the goal is to bring out your natural attractiveness. Don't make being what you were the goal. You're better than that! Make attractiveness your goal.

Use conditioner on your hair. Help it to shine again and help it to look great again—regardless of whether you choose to wear it long or short.

It is very important that you take care of your skin. Use plenty of moisturizing cream on your face—night and day! Keeping your skin supple is an on-going process. Take it seriously.

Now, ladies, I know almost all of you have been applying make-up all your lives, but knowing that I'm still going to make the following suggestion—Get a make-over. Don't protest. Just do it.

You're probably using the same color make-up and lipstick that you used 30 or more years ago.

It's time for a change!

There is the old prayer, "Lord, grant me the strength to change the things I can change and the serenity to accept the things I cannot change—and the wisdom to know the difference between the two." This prayer should be uttered by every woman as she considers how to take care of her face and body during her retirement years.

Our faces and bodies change. We cannot do all that much about those changes. However, we do not have to stand idly by and pretend that we can't do anything. We can

There is a growing trend toward cosmetic surgery in the United States. Both men and women have been taking advantage of the skills of plastic surgeons in taking years from their appearance. Eye lifts. Face lifts. Liposuction. These are all procedures varying in complexity, but can produce dramatic results.

I've seen many men and women after surgery and I am constantly amazed at how wonderful they look. My mother's girlfriend just turned 75. A few months ago, she had plastic surgery on her face. The results were most gratifying! She looks fantastic!

I should add that she is currently dating again. A younger man.

Men, if you've been hating your thinning hair (or bald spots) for years, do something about it. Hair weaving. Hair pieces. Plugs.

There's no reason to shrug your shoulders as if nothing can be done. A great deal can be done.

Go for it! Although, I believe bald men are sexy!

Few things brighten a day like a smile. However, if you've been reluctant to smile because of your teeth—do something about it. Teeth whiteners. Bonding. Even braces are available to mature adults. Don't go another day without a smile!

Look good, feel good. If you think you're overweight (notice I said if you think you're overweight. Self image is the essence of beauty!) then consider going on a diet. However, before you begin a diet or exercise program, speak with your doctor or a nutritionist. Significant lifestyle changes should be approached intelligently.

Once you get the go ahead—do it!

The same advice is vital for those of you anxious to begin an exercise program. Virtually everyone can engage in exercise—from walking to canoeing to skiing to marathons. However, someone who has never been much of an exerciser shouldn't decide to run the marathon right away.

New exercise—and significant changes in exercise routines—should be discussed with your doctor. However, the bottom line is that you should exercise. Be active.

If you're going to begin an exercise program, invest in the right equipment, whether that's shoes, outfits, bats, balls or tennis racquets. And invest in a quality instructor! He can guide you to the appropriate machine or level of exercise.

Too much too soon ends up being counterproductive in the long run. Sore muscles. Aching joints. Burn-out. None of these contribute to long-term programs. And it is exactly a long-term program that you're after. Long-term because you are going to live a long, healthy, active life.

Stick with your instructor for at least eight weeks. Then you can go off on your own, confident that you understand your range of ability and that you're comfortable with the equipment you'll be using.

"But Shirley, how will I know when I'm in the right exercise program?"

The answer to that is straightforward. You'll know you're in the right program when, after a few short weeks, you begin to notice a change in yourself—not just your weight and body, but in your energy level, your sleep patterns and your appetite.

Your concentration too.

One of the things I tell people about appearance is, Brain Power.

"Brain power?" they ask. "What does brain power have to do with how a person looks?"

Simple. The light behind someone's eyes is the result of the fire burning within them. That's the result of keeping their hearths and minds active. Brain power.

Keep your brain razor sharp by taking a course in ceramics, wood carving, photography, history...whatever!

What is true with your body is true with your brain—use it or lose it!

The more you use it, the more you can appreciate one of the real bonuses of feeling good—you get to give your husband/wife, children, grandchildren and friends plenty of hugs. We all need hugs, both to get them and to give them. When you're feeling good—healthy and attractive—you are anxious to give those hugs.

There is nothing "academic" about this. Hugs, as far as I know, have never been the subject of a study. There is no statistical analysis for hugs. However, I have reams and reams of anecdotal evidence to prove my point.

I have been married to my most wonderful husband for 30 years and we give each other hugs every day. When my three beautiful sons were babies, I used to kiss and hug them every day. Not only did it do wonders for my own emotions, it was good for them.

If I could go back and marry Richard again. If I could raise my three sons again...if I had the choice to do it all over again, I would in a second! I loved every moment of it—the good and the bad.

Family is the world to me. Family should be the center of everyone's life. It is that family love that makes the world work.

Think seriously about the direction your life is taking. "Try it you'll like it." What's age got to do with it?

"Retirement." Just what does that mean today? It means playtime, relaxation. Getting to know the good life. No pressures, no stress, no alarm clocks. Retirement - you want it. Just make up your mind to do it and the good life will start!

The sooner you decide to take the plunge, the sooner you'll look and feel great! There is so much to do and to enjoy!

Try an adult community. They are full of fascinating things. I know, I have enjoyed chatting with a lot of pals who are enjoying the good life. Isn't it nice to finally have the time to do all you promised yourself. It's not as late as you think!

Who said, "Adventure is just for the young?" Come on now, the clock is ticking, it's time to have fun! Be young at heart. Hurry, buy yourself golf clubs, a tennis racquet or exercise equipment.

It's time to take charge of your life and enjoy. What's age got to do with it! Be happy.

"Shirley, everything you're saying makes such good sense," my friend Evelyn said to me the other day. "But how do I know when I'm ready to retire, when I'm ready for a change?"

"Evelyn, you know I don't deal in the abstract. I like the concrete. I think there are signs that any of us could spot that would let us know what our mental state is. But if you want to know when you've reached a point where you'd benefit from an active adult community, just examine your activities and behavior."

"How so?"

I shrugged. "For example, does the 7-11 clerk know you by your first name?"

Evelyn smiled sheepishly. "What's wring with that?"

"Nothing is wrong with it. But it means that you're spending a bit too much time at the local 7-11 and that means you're not spending enough time doing the things you should be doing—like having fun."

"Okay, I get your point."

Chapter Three
Retirement

Retired adults. God bless them all!

Many are scared and fearful of retirement. When the big day comes to retire, adults panic. They ask, What's going to happen now? Where do I go from here? What's it like in the retirement communities today? Could I be happy?

There comes a time in your life when you can finally take control of your life, and it frightens you. I can assure you, there are no risk factors in retirement today. It is a positive move! It is a celebration!

If your life was like being on a race track, you'll love retirement.

Be aware, "Age is just a number."

The benefits of retiring are so rewarding. It will add ten more healthy years to your life. Stress is cut out completely.

Take a sensible approach to retirement. Examine your priorities. What's important to you and your partner? Is it being close to your children? Or is it important what area you live in?

If you are now looking for a retirement community to live in, you are headed to a rewarding new lifestyle and you don't know it yet.

Be philosophical about changes in your life. Speak openly to your partner about your needs. Share your ideas together. The changes in the home environment will be a plus. You will be enjoying happy days now.

I thought for a second, "All right, Saturday night doesn't mean anything special to you anymore."

Evelyn frowned but then she smiled. "Do you remember how people looked forward to Saturday night, how it was almost magical?"

"Of course I do."

"You can't expect it to be special like that still," Evelyn said, somewhat defensively.

"Not in the same way, of course not. But it *should* be special. Even if it seems arbitrary, you should have a night you look forward to, a 'stepping out' night."

"I suppose you're right," she conceded.

"Something more special, by the way, than the Saturday night line-up on the television."

Evelyn laughed softly.

"Another thing has to do with following through on plans. For instance, if you say that you're going to sign up for an exercise class—but never do."

Evelyn seemed to dismiss the comment with the wave of her hand. "But everyone does that. It's like a New Year's resolution. No one ever really expects to keep their resolutions."

"Maybe not, but if you promise yourself that you're going to make a change in your life and then don't... well, that's one of the signs that you're ready for a community that invites those kinds of changes."

"If you don't seem to be having fun anymore, it's time that you look honestly at yourself and figure out a way to make a change for the better."

"Fun," Evelyn said with a gentle snort. "I haven't heard anyone have fun since I was a girl."

"I have," I said, almost boastfully. "Lots of people. They're having the time of their lives."

"Really?"

"Absolutely," I said firmly. "You know, we talked about not looking forward to Saturday night. Well, when I speak with people and they don't seem to always remember whether it's Monday or Friday—if they kind of lose the weekend in the blur of days—then they're ready for a change."

"If they're confused..."

"It's not confusion," I pointed out. "It's letting yourself become inactive, letting your mind and body go on retirement."

"Retirement doesn't mean putting your mind and body out to pasture. It means finally be free from the relentless time clock, to be free to do things that you want to do, that you've been looking forward to doing for years, it means cutting down on your responsibilities so that you can enjoy life more."

"The people I work with are having fun and they're not confused as to the reason why. They're surrounded by interesting and interested people, people who are active, who want to stay active..."

"All this talk about staying active is tiring me out," Evelyn observed, half in jest.

"You know the funniest thing about it? Active people sleep better. That's the truth. Sometimes when I meet people who have an interest in the community, I ask them only one question and, based on their answer, they sign up immediately."

"One question? Really? What's the question?"

"Do you stay asleep all night?"

Ask yourself how you feel about your daily activities. Are you bored? Are there all sorts of things you would like to be doing, but you aren't?

Now that the kids are grown, do you feel that it's your time for fun, but your not sure what you want to do?

Everyday I talk with people who know they're not satisfied, but don't know what to do about it. They're not comfortable with making changes, because they only know about what they'll be leaving behind. It's funny how you can be unhappy with something, but you cling to it because you don't know what else is out there.

People in their fifties and sixties are starting an entirely new phase in their lives. They're going to have many healthy, active years ahead and they have to develop new ideas about how to spend all that time. After years of hard work, raising a family and dedicating yourself to everybody else, it can be tough to concentrate on your own needs and wishes. Trust me, it's only hard at the beginning.

Most people can get an entirely new outlook simply by taking those first few steps to try something new—just for the fun of it. Go find the classes, the clubs, trips or sports programs and get involved. While it sounds simple, I know it can also be a bit scary. I see it all the time: The woman who has always been a wonderful cook, then starts as a total beginner in a wok class—the tennis player who tries golf for the first time—the new coin-collector who joins a club of "experts."

It may be a long time since you've been a "beginner" at anything, but all the best things start at the beginning. After the first couple of times, it becomes easier and easier to put yourself in new situations. And, it's amazing how you can start with one painting class or volunteer group and then discover so many other things to try.

The people I work with start out wondering how they're going to be spending all their free time and end up saying to me, "There aren't enough hours in the day to do everything I want. I never imagined I would be playing computer bridge; on a softball team again; designing my own jewelry; developing my own photographs; doing water aerobics, etc."

When you find yourself wanting more, that means you're ready to make those changes. There are all sorts of new beginnings for you to make. And, you owe yourself all the good times that are out there to be enjoyed.

To this end, I share with you my list of twelve things to help get the most physically out of everyday and to thereby be most happy.

1. Wake up and before getting out of bed point your toes and stretch your arms over your head. Stretch, stretch, stretch.

2. Turn on the radio to your favorite radio station playing "your music." Sing along. Dance. Enjoy!

3. Take a fifteen minute bike ride or walk.

4. Take a class in something you always wanted to learn, but never had the time.

5. Eat lunch out.

6. Buy a good book—and read it!

7. Call your best friend if you have one. If you don't—GET ONE!

8. Decorate your home to whatever season it is. Buy flowers and holiday decorations.

9. Plan a trip.

10. Love life. After all, it's the only one you've got.

11. Live for the moment.

12. Buy a Mercedes.

Okay, you can get away with only the first eleven.

Chapter Four
Retirement and Romance

Although I've spoken quite a bit about the "retirement years" many active adults have found that they have put off retirement. Active adults tend to work longer. Employers recognize that mature adults enjoy much more experience than young people and that they are very dependable. That is why so many companies and corporations are going out of their way to actually recruit mature workers.

That was the case with Mary and Bill. They were working beyond their "normal" retirement.

Mary, 69 years young, and Bill, 70, met at a computer company where they were both working.

Both Mary and Bill had been married between 35 and 40 years. They had raised their children into responsible adulthood and then, after their contributions and lifetimes of joys and sorrows, had found themselves alone.

"It's very hard when your mate passes away," Bill explained. "You lose your lover, your wife—or husband—and most importantly, the best friend you've got."

"We were both very fortunate. Our friends were very supportive and our children, God bless them, have been there whenever we've needed them, but no matter what anyone else does, there's no way that they can plug that huge hole in your life and heart."

"Just can't do it."

Mary agreed. "You just keep your head up best you can and keep going. It's hard. Really hard. There are lots of times that you really believe that your life ended with your mate's."

"Going on alone is so hard."

When I asked them if it was easy for them to get together, Bill chuckled. "Depends what you mean by easy. I wanted to ask Mary out for about a year before I finally approached her."

"Of course, I felt the exact same way. I wanted to go out with Bill but I couldn't say yes. Guilt. Fear. I don't know what. I just couldn't accept the fact that a person I was attracted to was attracted to me."

Fortunately, Bill wouldn't give up. He kept trying until Mary finally relented.

"I couldn't help it," he explained. "Sometimes I felt like a damned fool. Asking her out. Flirting with her. I was scared I was making her uncomfortable and even more scared than I was."

"It was like being a kid again."

"I was so attracted to Mary. I never, never thought I would feel that way again. After my wonderful wife was gone, I thought my life was over. I didn't think I'd ever get so lucky twice in my lifetime."

"I was so glad he kept after me," Mary confessed. "How could I ever resist such a handsome man for long?" Then she laughed sweetly.

With Valentine's Day coming up, Bill took the opportunity to seek me out and show me the card he'd written for Mary.

"Are you sure you want me to read this?" I asked him.

"I'm sure. I need to get a woman's perspective on it." He handed me the card and then watched me. As he did, a tear formed down his eye.

I glanced down to the card and began to read. What he had written had come directly from the heart.

> If it were not for you, Mary, I think I would have faded away.
>
> You made my life worth getting up in the mornings again.
>
> The happiness you have brought me has filled the hole in my heart again.
>
> I look forward to each bright day again.

I love you and your warmth and beautiful
ways, your sincerity and genuine
honesty

Will you marry me?

"It's perfect," I told Bill, my own eyes moist with emotion.

Bill took the card back and looked down at it. "I hope she thinks so."

A few days later, I saw Mary and Bill together and I approached them. I looked first at Bill and raised my eyebrows in a questioning glance. He smiled and placed his arm around Mary's shoulders.

"Tell, Shirley," he urged softly.

"The card?" she asked, glancing up into his eyes.

He nodded.

"It was magical, wasn't it? I just... I was just so overwhelmed. Of course I said I would marry him. But," she added with a slight frown, "there are so many complications." Then she turned to Bill. "We'll work them out though. Every last one."

When Mary looked back at me, her eyes were steady. "The government is just going to have to change the system for older, mature adults. We are living much longer now and because we all have to think about what will happen if we are left alone

—and maybe meet someone special like I did and want to get married."

"But what's the problem?" I asked.

"Before we can get married, one of us—if not both of us—will have to sell our home because we would lose out on the first $125,000 tax exemption." "And, of course, there's the children. They worry about their inheritance! No kidding, they don't understand that mom or dad has fallen in love and want to get married. Romance is only for them. We're supposed to sit around and watch television."

Mary sighed. "No, we're supposed to sit around and do nothing, otherwise, we could even lose our Social Security pensions—which we've worked for.

"I'll tell you, getting married at our age is more complicated than you would think. We have to work out a lot of things." Then her expression became firm. "But we don't care."

"That's right," Bill said. "We're in love and we want to be together. And we're not interested in just living together to make it easier on everyone else.

"That's not our way. It's important to us to do what is important to us."

It seemed so unbelievable that older, mature adults would have to worry about falling in love again. But to face what they had to face... it seemed unfair. Still, just like love with the young, love with the mature adult tends to persevere.

"Love will find a way," Mary acknowledged softly. "We have no doubt about that."

"Just so long as you keep me up to date on the progress," I told them. I wanted so many good things for them. The were so determined—and deservedly so. I couldn't wait to learn what they would do.

A short time later I learned that both Bill and Mary were selling their houses and moving into an active adult community "together"

"So long as we're together," Bill said, "That's the important thing."

Chapter Five
Not Everything is so Simple

One of the really wonderful things about dealing with older, mature adults is that they have lived through so many experiences. "Earned our stripes," one of my friends calls it.

One woman I know, a fascinating, strong and vibrant woman, has chosen not to have cosmetic surgery to remove any of the wrinkles from her face. "I've earned each and every one of these," she claims. "I'm not giving even one away."

The joy and strength behind her blue-green eyes makes her one of the most attractive women I've ever met.

It's true, what she says, we have earned each and every wrinkle. Whether we want to keep the wrinkle or not. And, with our experience, we know that love is not always so straightforward as for Bill and Mary.

Take Doris and Bruce, both 65 years young. They were married directly out of high school and they struggled through 20 years of a difficult marriage. After they divorced, they both remarried, but neither of their second marriages was successful.

Doris and Bruce met again a few years later

and found that the "old magic" was still there. They remarried in 1987—only to divorce again in 1990.

They remarried a third time in 1993.

Who said it was easy? But it can work. Doris and Bruce are living in an active adult community.

"The people we've met and the things we can do—they make all the difference in the world," Bruce said.

"This time, we're going to stay together," Doris added.

Chapter Six
Falling In Love

Some people react with surprise when they learn that older adults "fall in love." They say that it's not... seemly. But the fact is, more and more mature adults are falling in love and planning their weddings and finding new issues to go up against.

Anyone who believes that love goes "out the window" at 60 or 65 is in for a real shock. Buying homes, buying new furniture, looking for interior decorators... planning for the future. It's happening all the time. And it's great!

Are there problems? Of course. Difficult ones. Complex ones. Problems that would overwhelm younger people falling in love. Mature adults have a lot of "baggage." They don't have to worry about young children, they have to worry about older children, children who are adults themselves.

These adult children worry about their parents. They worry about how their decisions will affect them emotionally and financially.

Let me give all mature adults one piece of advice—you can't worry about your children when you believe you have the chance to be happy again.

You've got to go for it!

Children who are appalled to see their mature parents dressed in anything other than black or gray don't appreciate that older adults have the same desires as younger adults.

I've seen grandmothers and grandfathers look quite striking and sexy through their 60s and 70s. No, they have not resorted to tight fitting jeans or see-through anythings. What they have done is put their wardrobe together with intelligence, charm and wit.

Sure, older people see their bodies change, but with exercise and attention to diet, it's not unreasonable to get that "second look" again.

The first rule in being attractive is letting that inner light shine through. Be happy! The best thing you can do to be attractive is to SMILE!!

A smile is the first thing you should put on every morning and the last thing you take off at night.

Jeannie, in her late 60s, wears a long pony-tail. Barbara, Joyce and Lorraine color their hair. They are all beautiful. The hair coloring takes ten years off the ladies. Each has gone to the trouble of finding a good hairdresser. A bad hairdresser tends to make a woman look as if she's wearing a cap.

A woman wants her hair to move and be sexy.

Chapter Seven
Let's Give 'em Something to Talk About!

People always ask me, Do people date in retirement communities? Do people ever get married after they retire if they move into a retirement community? It's so funny. Life doesn't stop because you retire. When you're living in an active adult community, you are bound to meet a lot of new people. Life goes on, no matter what age you are. Of course people date!

I see them all day and evening long, holding hands, eating ice cream cones together, laughing and just having fun. Why not? Yes, is my answer to the question. Yes!

Artie, a single man, dropped by to chat with me. Artie has always been a pleasure to see and speak to. However, he was adamant in claiming that he would always be single. "Maybe if I met the right lady, I'd get married again..."

This day, there was a special sparkle in Artie's eyes. "Shirley," he said, "you're not going to believe this but I was driving through the gates as I always do and I got to know the guard. He knew I was single and he asked me if I wanted to meed a nice lady, a friend of his girlfriend's mother. I said, "Sure, why not?"

"I called her up to make a date to meet her. When I saw her for the first time, I knew right off she was for me!"

Judy felt the same way about Artie. They've met each other's families and everyone seems to really like everyone else.

"She's changed my life," Artie claimed. "We are decorating our home. She is so full of life! Never a dull moment. We're going to Florida on our honeymoon," he said, shaking his head in amazement at his good fortune. "I'm 73 years young and I'm planning my honeymoon!"

"I just want to say you're only as young as you think!"

Although it still comes as a shock to a lot of people, you *are* allowed to fall in love when you're a mature adult. You can still make out. And God forbid!, you can still think about and engage in sex.

The funny thing is, mature adults seem just as shocked as young people. Did they really believe that they'd live to be 100 without ever having sex?

As much as your grandchildren love you, do you really think they worry about your sex life? They don't.

I've interviewed over a thousand active adults and often I discuss intimate matters with them. The answers that I get are really quite enlightening.

One woman, 68 years young, said that she thought her world ended when her husband of 43 years died. "There would never be anyone who could take his place," she said. "I told myself I would get by on my own—with the help of my children."

However, on a cold, windy and icy February morning, she found herself having to go out in that weather, but she needed to have something in the house in case the weather turned out even worse.

"It must have been Fate that got me out of the house on that day," she said. "Going to the store that day was going to change my life forever."

"I couldn't reach the cans of string beans and I thought to myself, Why don't the stores understand that older people can't reach so high and put items lower for us."

"I tried and I tried to reach the cans of beans when like an angel from heaven, a gentle hand reached up and grabbed the can for me."

"Here you are, toots," the voice said, handing me the can. "I saw you were struggling so I thought I might be of some help." Well, you can imagine how I felt! I wished I'd fixed my hair and put on some lipstick that day.

"But you know, it didn't matter. Not one bit. Will introduced himself to me and we talked for about 20 minutes. It was the funniest thing. It turned out we lived on the same block and we'd never seen each other before."

"Will was a widower. We both had so much in common," she smiled. "I noticed the twinkle in his big, blue eyes right away. At first, I didn't know what I was feeling and then when I did I was shocked. I never thought Id be attracted to another man, but there I was feeling like I'd been swept off my feet."

"We started dating. I tell you, I felt like a schoolgirl again. Walking on a cloud. It was glorious. After a time, we decided to get married. We went to Paris on our honeymoon after a small wedding."

"My grandson gave me away. It was so... so moving. My daughter cried, she was so happy for me. And, oh yes," she added, looking me directly in the eye, "we have great sex. Love can happen if you let it."

"Of course, I *never* complain about the string bean cans being too high in the grocery store anymore!"

Love and sex do continue for almost every mature adult. Is it the same as when they were 20? Usually not, but that doesn't change the power and beauty of it.

One man, 70 years young, told me, "Sex isn't like an earthquake anymore. It's more like a tremor." Another man, 75 told me he enjoys sex only once a month, but that it's great.

A female friend of mine, 72 years young, tells me she dreams about sex quite a bit, but she's afraid to do anything about it. "I think I'm a virgin again by now!"

"Sex is better after the kids move out," one man, 57 years young, proclaimed. "You can scream and make as much noise as you want and no one will hear you!"

When I asked the question of one 60 year

young man, he laughed. "I like to chase her around the table until I catch her—usually about twice a week."

"Slower, but better," one man told me.

A poll I took at the Men's and Women's Singles Club resulted in the following information:

65% of women like sex more after retirement

35% of men like sex more after retirement.

Men like sex, but not as often as women.

Men love to be in love, have a partner, enjoy home-made meals, a clean house, be busy, to talk, to see their children and grandchildren, travel.

Women love to eat out, no cleaning anymore, to see their children and grandchildren, enjoy their quiet time, friends, dancing, nesting, being busy.

Perhaps the cutest story about mature adults and sex comes from Mary.

"Thanksgiving was coming and my son was coming. Now, our house is a lovely size—not big by any stretch. Two bedrooms."

"Thinking about his visit, I was worried about the noise we might make in our bedroom. After being married for 40 years, you would think we were doing something wrong! But my husband and I still worry every time my children come to visit."

"The first thing my son said when he arrived was, 'Mom, Dad, I guess you don't care where we sleep because you haven't done anything for years now.' Of course, he meant sex."

"I wish I could tell him how active we are. We love not having to worry about anyone walking in on us. Yes, we would like to say, just because our bodies don't look like the bodies of 20 year olds, our minds still *think* like 20 year olds."

"Older people want everyone to know—It's about time you know we don't think any different than we did when we were younger. Our minds think young always—just as our imaginations imagine young!"

"We don't have any control over our bodies aging. We keep in shape. We exercise. But we can't help the breakdown of aging. But we do enjoy sex. Please don't ever take that away from us."

"It's time people sit back and listen to what we have to say. We like sex as much as you do. We fall in love too. We enjoy the first date again. The kissing and the hugging. Flowers sent to us.

Romance is always important. And we love someone caring for us, in addition to our children of course."

"A mate. Yes, that's right. And if we're not married, we like having a boyfriend or a girlfriend."

Chapter Eight
Transitions/The Four Fears

"Change is hard."

I read that once in a book, although I cannot now remember the name of the book. However, the sentiment is right on target. Although change can be exciting, it is difficult. The greater the change, the greater the difficulty.

Because of this, retirement is a very difficult time. Frightening. I try to be very clear that retirement is just the beginning, the beginning of a period of life that is active, exciting and wonderful. Still, not to acknowledge the difficulty of the transition would be unfair.

Most people confront four main fears in retirement.

1. The feeling that, with retirement, life is over. Even to utter the word "retire" seems to be a capitulation, a concession.

2. The scared, empty feeling when that last child, the baby, moves out. Suddenly, a fun damental way of defining oneself is gone. No longer "parent" in the immediate sense.

3. The fear of selling one's home. There's no easy way to leave the home where you've

been living for 30 or 40 years. "Home." It's not just a house. Not just a place. Every room, every corner is fraught with memories and meanings. Leaving it seems to mean leaving everything *but* the memories.

4. The fear of moving to a new area. How far should one go from one's loved ones? New friends. New stores. New doctors.

So many things change. Fundamental changes. So much to be frightened of...

However, as in most things, our fears are the result of what we don't know. Let me enlighten you to the reality of retirement today, in the 1990s!

You've got the bug, you're seriously thinking that the time has come. You're thinking of selling your home and moving into an adult community.

The first thing you should do is VISIT a lot of communities and see what kind of home you would like. Do you want a smaller or larger home? There are all kinds available. And, when you're looking at the homes, be sure to keep "lifestyle" in mind. Check out the Club House and the Calendar of Events.

After a few visits to different places, consider yourself a "serious" buyer. Return to the places you liked during the day and meet some of the residents who live there. They are your best resources for learning the truth about a community. A brochure or an employee is supposed to paint the perfect pic ture. You want the real picture.

Residents never lie. Remember, the person you're talking to actually lives in the community. If he or she appears excited or happy, you can believe that you will most likely be happy there too.

People are living much healthier and longer lives today than ever before. Retirement at 55, 60 or 65 still means 20 or 30 years of active and pleasurable life.

Twenty or 30 years!

"What will I do?"

"How do I do it?"

"Where shall I live?"

"Do I want a large or small community?"

Everyone tells me that they want to live with "young-thinking" adults. Well, people retiring today will have many, many years to enjoy retirement. So, do you go into an adult community?

After all, you want to retire, but you don't want to go into an "old age home."

But you don't have to. Retirement today is just another change in lifestyle. Life moves forward in stages. You go from one stage to the next. Each stage is great! Enjoy each one of them!

The fear of moving into a new area is a very real one. There are new relationships to be formed. New friends. New neighbors. New doctors. Even

new shopping centers.

"I'm used to my area. I've lived there for so many years. How will I get around someplace else? I don't drive."

"Where are the houses of worship? The churches and synagogues?"

These are the questions everyone has. You'll be pleasantly surprised to find how anxious your new neighbors will be to help you answer your questions—and get over your fears. They have already gone through this transition. they understand what is difficult about it. They'll be more than happy to exchange notes with you.

You're sure to find a new doctor you like and trust, a new friend, a new neighbor—and a new shopping center!

Getting around is never a problem. Adult communities have transportation available <u>if you want it</u>. Some residents prefer to drive their own cars.

"I was worried about leaving my home," one resident told me. "But when I looked at the pros and cons, there was no question about what I wanted to do. I wanted to be free of the maintenance and upkeep of my home. I wanted to be free of the tax burden—and the responsibilities."

His community provided transportation, 24 hour security, the opportunity to meet new people his own age.

"There was so much to do," he said. "It was overwhelming at first. I was like a kid in a candy shop!"

The change is good for your physical and mental health. You become more, not less, active. Your children will like that as well. They will be proud of your independence.

Yes, change is hard. It is also exciting. Retirement is a new adventure, one that can lead to a refreshing new outlook on life. You'd never have had the opportunity to change your outlook if you'd remained in your home.

Move on. Move on! Try new things. A new, active neighborhood makes trying new things easy.

As one resident shared with me, "I never believed I could be this happy and content."

Change is hard. But the rewards can be so magnificent.

Chapter Nine
My Baby is Moving Out

They don't call it an "empty nest" for nothing.

If you were a mother who stayed home to take care of your children, who enjoyed the work of raising a family, you know the feeling. If you were a working mother, constantly on the run, dashing around, trying to make every minute count, you know the feeling.

Try to remember the time your own mother told you to enjoy your children because they grow up fast and you asked, "When?" because for you, the time couldn't come fast enough.

Well, it came—and went.

Borrowing the car keys. Asking for money. The stereo blasting. Football games, soccer games baseball games... Good times. Hectic times. Family times.

Now the bedrooms are empty. Well yes, it is an empty nest. But usually not for long. Young people go to college and then come back. You're glad to see them of course. But do you find yourself telling yourself that you liked the peace and quiet too?

Don't worry. If you move to an active adult community, your children will visit even more because they will love your new lifestyle and they'll want to enjoy it with you.

Retirement isn't being put out to pasture, it's being able to get up early for your tee-off.

I keep hearing that when the grandchildren visit, they don't want to go home. They love staying with their grandparents and enjoying all the amenities the community has to offer.

"Can I come back next week?"

Grandparents chuckle happily. After all, the grandchildren had been with them for two weeks already.

Your new lifestyle will have so much to offer everyone in your family. You'll be proud of your new friends and your new community.

And your family will enjoy:
Swimming—at certain hours.
Playing tennis.
Playing bocci.
Playing shuffleboard, horseshoes, basketball.

Can they do all these things at your old house now?

Chapter Ten
This Old House, Selling It

Of course you're going to miss your home. You've lived in it for 20, 30, 40 years. Missing anything makes you feel sad. But stop and think for a moment. It's not really the house you're going to miss. It's the memories you have of the things that happened in it. The memories travel with you! In fact, they're already packed and ready to move.

Moving will give you the chance to create new memories. Your children will be proud of you and will be impressed with your new surroundings. Your independence will have a tremendous impact on them.

Don't ever be afraid of changing. You will be having new experiences with brand new, happy memories. More memories than you ever thought you could have in your new home. And all without the burdens of the old house.

No more maintenance bills. No more repairs that never seemed to end. No more fixing a crack or painting a room or patching a patio when you should be out enjoying life.

No more cutting the lawn.

Sell your lawn mower and don't look back!

Don't you remember that first big snowfall every year? What about the minute *after* you were taken up with the wonder, the beauty, the serenity of it? You know, the minute when you climbed out of bed, knowing that you had to begin shoveling and snow blowing?

Sell the shovel. Sell the snow blower. You won't be needing it anymore!

Look at the beautiful homes in the new retirement communities—every bit as elegant as those in your neighborhood.

You lose so very, very little and you gain so very, very much! New, happy memories. New, wonderful friends. Caring, warm, friendly.

Let go of your fears. There is so much joy and... and fun awaiting you!

Sell your home a bit at a time. Sell the lawn mower. The paint brushes. The snow blower. The rakes. The putty knives. The hammer and screwdriver.

It won't be long before you realize that the things that you think are holding you to your old house are really not holding you at all. Set yourself free. You are the only one holding yourself back!

There is so much to look forward to.

Chapter Eleven
Aging

Okay, you say, everything sounds fine and good, but no amount of "sugar coating" will change the fact that you're aging. You're right. You're aging. So is the baby just born and the child entering adolescence. So is the 24 year old woman who just became pregnant with her first child.

So, what do we mean when we say "aging?" I've been with mature adults, day by day, and I've witnessed the actual process in a lot of people. Here's what I've observed:

Starting from, say, 48 to 90—yes, to 90—physical changes occur. When I talk about the aging process, I'm talking about physical aging. The "outside."

In many ways, our bodies are like machines. Just like any other machine, it has to be maintained or it won't run the way we'd like it to. You can't abuse it—neither by overuse or neglect.

Okay, so what are the physical changes I've seen? These changes begin with aches and pains. There is a gradual slowing down. However, in spite of this, you continue to enjoy a great many things. Bike riding. Dancing, etc. The mind—and your ability to enjoy what you do—does not change.

Sure, there are those who are annoyed because they can't ride their bike as far or as fast as when they were 20. Some people are annoyed because they can't play basketball on a par with Magic Johnson.

The point is simple, enjoying life demands that you live it to the fullest *within the parameters of you ability*. Enjoying a bike ride of ten miles can be at least as pleasurable when you're 55 as riding 30 miles when you're 20.

Mature adults have the same thoughts and feelings as they did throughout their lives. Inside, you are the same. Outside, the body begins to show the wears and tears of the years. But the wears and tears don't make you old. No, what makes you old is when your heart shows the wears and tears, when you stop being young at heart.

Mature adults I've met tend to age slower when they don't think about their age. They don't think, "Oh my, I'm X years old. I can't think/act like that anymore."

Sure, we reach a point where it seems we are fighting the genes we inherited. We lose our hair. Our weight shifts. We seem to lose muscle mass more quickly and have to work harder to get it back.

Adult communities are not, God forbid, senior citizen homes. What a horrible title, senior citizen. No mature adult I know likes it. They say it makes them <u>feel</u> old. Besides, adult communities are for people from age 48 and up. Few people I know would—or should—consider 48 to be old.

I've met 30 year olds who look and act old and I've known many, many 75 year young who look and act 30 years younger.

There is a certain grace that comes with staying in tune with life. We all go through transitions in life. We must learn to accept them and enjoy them. The brain and the heart must stay young.

It is the heart and the mind that keep us young. What's age got to do with it!

No one can be isolated and remain "young." We need to be around other people. We need to be part of the flow of life, no matter what age we are. Alone, we age fast. Together, we age more slowly. More gracefully. More enjoyable.

We do not get older. We get better. It's a question of attitude. Aging is in the mind even more than the body.

Chapter Twelve
Retirement has Changed

Time was when grandparents went to bed early. Now they dance to the tunes of their youth 'till the wee hours of the morning. Time was, grandpops drive big cars—always blue or beige two-toners. Now you see them buzzing about in smart little sports cars.

Time was when grandmoms wore big, flowered house dresses. Now they wear brightly colored warm-up suits, sneakers, shorts, bleached-out sweatshirts and stylish swimsuits all the while reading publications like, "I'd Rather Be Over The Hill Than Under It!"

Time was when grandpops were couch potatoes. Now they're running out the door to go to baseball practice, bowling or golfing—or maybe they're enjoying lunch with their own "lunch bunch."

Time was when grandmoms and grandpops would sleep late because they couldn't sleep at night. Now, they wake up early to attend a tennis clinic, practice shuffleboard or go for their daily walk. Oh, and sleeping at night is no problem for most now that they have an active daily routine.

Time was, grandmoms and grandpops would

sit by the phone, hoping to hear from their children and grandchildren. Now they have answering machines so they can catch the calls while they're out having a good time.

Time was when grandmoms would call and ask if they could have the grandchildren visit with them. Now, the grandchildren call and ask if they can come to visit!

Time was when grandmoms did all the housework while grandpop watched the television. No more. Now grandpop is helping with the wash, the housecleaning and the shopping. He's helping to cook too. Even taking cooking lessons!

Time was when grandmoms and grandpops never dated. Now, some of them are off to see a New York play and have dinner with their date.

Time was...

It seems so long ago. Almost quaint. Now, you can pick grandmoms and grandpops out in a crowd. They're the ones holding hands, helping someone, sharing an idea, smiling, laughing and telling a beautiful story about their lifestyle before retirement. Showing pictures of their family and sharing their new lifestyle.

Grandmoms and grandpops can be trusted. They are honest, loving, helpful, intelligent, talented and very caring about their fellow human beings when the need comes up. If you get sick, look to them to knock on your door with a bowl of homemade chicken soup!

Chapter Thirteen
Are You Ready for a Change

So you think retirement would be boring? You wonder what it would really be like to be retired in the 1990s.

Wonder no more!

Living an active adult life is getting up in the morning and looking forward to a busy day. It's going to your refrigerator door to check out the Calendar of Events so you don't miss out on anything.

There is a new breed of active adults retiring today. You'll love being with them and sharing happy new memories. Retirement today means:

* never feeling alone

* having the freedom to do things you never had time for before

* being on constant vacation

* thinking young

* keeping fit; eating healthy

* having the feeling of excitement again. Like going to your first prom.

* seeing smiles on everyone's faces

* participating in activities and events you never thought you could

* never having to mow the lawn or shovel snow again

* having the best lifestyle

* enjoying life to the fullest

* putting your head on your pillow at night, happily exhausted and sleeping like a baby.

Retiring now means being unable to wait for the next day because you know that it will be filled with fun and activities. It means having to listen to your answering machine to get your messages because you're always out having fun. It means having to decide *which* trip to go on, Atlantic City for the day or maybe Wildwood for the week...

I have worked with mature adults for over a decade. Thousands of wonderful people and I have come to know and appreciate them. I know that a broadcast of the Senior Golf tournament will bring in a crowd while younger pros won't excite much interest.

Arnold Palmer. Jack Nicklaus. Lee Trevino. They're a bit heavier and their hair is a bit thinner, but they still have that magic. They haven't lost the magic!

The golf pros were fooling around with each other—laughing and having fun. Frank Sinatra was crooning in the background.

What a success! And what a pleasure to see

more mature adults being recognized for their talents and abilities. The greatest strength those players had maintained was the fact that they'd stayed young at heart.

An active adult community encourages staying young at heart— without compromising anything about being older. There is not a single mature adult who does not talk about his or her children and grandchildren first. It is for this reason that I encourage retiring adults to buy a home with at least two bedrooms. They don't always believe me at first, but I tell them that they *will* get visitors. Lots of them.

The Club House is available for family get togethers and parties. Not long ago, I was able to see a precious scene—four generations together to celebrate a couple's 40th wedding anniversary.

The couple's grandson got up to make a speech that went like this, "I want to congratulate you, grandmom and grandpop, for loving each other so long. If it weren't for you, grandmom, I wouldn't be here. And if it weren't for you, grandpop, I wouldn't have had the chance to play shuffleboard all the time!"

Everyone laughed and cried at the same time. It was a perfect moment. Just perfect.

Not only is an active adult community wonderful for a person's immediate family, it is also the "extended" family of the community that is a benefit. When a resident is experiencing a tragedy, all I have to do is pick up the phone and I will have an army of adults asking, "What time am I needed?"

You're never alone. One resident recently

baked a delicious cake in her beautiful Club House so she could share her recipe with all the other residents. Such love and sharing. You're never alone —unless you want to be. If you want company and conversation, the Club House is just a short walk away.

If you stayed in your big house in the woods, you'd have to invite someone over to have the same situation. You shouldn't have to constantly plan just for some companionship.

Here, you have companionship just down the path!

Today's retired adults are willing to try new adventures, to try new experiences, to learn and to grow! They have the time and, most importantly, they have the desire.

Financially, today's retired adults are better off than their parents were because they've planned ahead. The have been looking forward to this phase of their lives. No one is looking for a "last" place to live. They are prudent buyers. They are planners. They consider how much space they will need. They want a two-car garage. They want an extra bedroom for their children and grandchildren.

They want to know what the community has to offer to them.

"This is it. I want it all and I won't settle for anything but the best!" is the sentiment that I'm hearing from a great many adults.

Don't waver. Don't keep wondering, "Is it time for me to retire?" Do it! You wouldn't be asking the questions if you weren't ready.

Retiring to an active adult community is like having a travel agent plan a trip—everything is taken care of in advance. All you have to do is ENJOY.

Don't worry about liking it. You WILL.

My mother is 75 years young and I can honestly say that there are times when she has more energy than I do. She is very pretty. Why, I've been asked if she was my sister.

She has always taken very good care of herself. She drives a sports car. She loves to dance and swim. She loves the beach. And, oh yes, she still dates.

She has a zest for life that would be admirable in someone half her age. Thanks to her, I've learned to enjoy everything life has to offer. She celebrates every holiday. She is enthusiastic and warm and caring.

Her grandchildren adore her. Her children love her. We think she is perfect—she has cherished her independence. Sometimes I think that is what has kept her so young, her independence.

In return for her attitude she gets to enjoy life.

Isn't it wonderful to live such a full and enriching life? Anyone can. You can. Just get with the program! Being able to be independent makes retiring in an active adult community very rewarding.

Active adult living opens the door to single adults too. You don't have to be afraid to live alone. The security is great—a phone call away.

"It sounds wonderful, Shirley. But, will I like it?"

Every new resident or potential resident has that doubt. All I can say is that, having met thousands of people who have come to live in an active adult community, the answer is a resounding, YES!

After a couple of weeks, I invariably hear:

"I should have done this years ago."

"I feel so much younger!"

"I'm so happy!"

If I could only share the enthusiasm behind these quotes, you would all understand so much better how fulfilling it is to retire to an active adult community.

"I love retirement. I have so many new friends to do things with."

"I thought I was young, but since the first day I moved in, I've loved it. You never get lonely."

"To us, this is the Fountain of Youth! Stick around and grow younger and younger. We love it!"

"When we go on vacation, we can't wait to come back home."

"We're having a ball. We need another day in

the week to do all we'd like to do."

"Until we moved, we never needed a calendar. Wish we could tell the whole world so they could be as happy as we are!"

"I think the security is great. I like all the activities."

"We love our new, exciting lifestyle."

"I feel free to ride my bike. I love the golf and tennis, too."

"The concept is so beautiful—what a wonderful life."

"We are so happy. We're having a ball!"

"I thought I'd miss my house I've been in for 35 years. But a house is just walls, it's the people who make it a home."

Do you hear the spirit? The enthusiasm? These people have worked all their lives and feel they deserve the best there is to offer in retirement. I agree. Don't you?

Many residents begin to take even better care of themselves once they move in. Exercise classes in the morning. Swimming. Biking. Hiking. Walking. Jogging. Tennis. Golf. Healthy meals. Classes to keep the mind exercised. Sun and fresh air. Good attitudes.

The first year in residence, you'll try and do *everything*! By the second year, you'll pick and choose, having found the combination of activities that feels right for you. That's the way it should be.

Retirement is a wonderful adventure. Like all adventures, there's learning and growth constantly taking place.

Enjoy the adventure!

The best is yet to come. And you've earned it! All you have to do is reach out and all the pain you are feeling, all the questions, will disappear. Give yourself the chance and the permission to "go for the gold!"

I have seen grandfathers playing tennis with the vigor and vitality of their partners—their grandsons! I have seen grandmothers walk into the Club House with their daughters, looking just as sexy!

I have seen the change in people. Let me ease your concerns if you are worried about retirement—you will be so busy that your children will have to buy you an answering machine just to make sure the messages arrive.

Open the doors on a new world and lifestyle.

You can be as busy as you like or just kick back and take it all in slowly.

You can bet your life you are going to live an active one. There is so much to do, see and learn.

The trick is to be independent. We all want that. Curiously, we have some people moving into adult communities and buying bigger houses so that *their* parents can live with them.

This is a wonderful thing. However, often the

younger active adults must find a "sitter" to help their parents be active too.

I dearly wish there was something like "Sonset"—Senior Sitting—to help older citizens maintain their independence and their integrity. It's time. In fact, it's long overdue.

We need to insure dignity and independence throughout all the stages of life. After all, it wasn't so long ago that you were glad to still be alive at 50. Now, 50 is young. Sixty is young. Seventy, even 75.

I see adults dating, dancing, laughing—and getting married—into their 80s!

The world is changing. Change with it!

Go for the gold!

Chapter Fourteen
Even More Changes Ahead

As much as "retirement" has changed in the last few decades, there are more changes ahead. In fact, the entire concept of retiring is in flux. More and more active adults are working part-time or continuing to own their own businesses. They are living 30 to 35 years longer than the generation before them. With all those prosperous years ahead, they want to continue having their "hands in the till."

More and more, we will see children (themselves, mature adults) bringing their parents to live with them in a retirement community. Rather than leave them to live alone, they will opt to have them in the same, wonderfully active community that they had chosen for themselves.

After all, if they are living longer and longer, it stands to reason that their parents are as well.

Even while some people continue with their hands in the till, the average retirement age will continue to drop due to corporate buyouts and attractive severance packages. Add to this the fact that we will be living well into our 100s, thanks to eating right, exercising and the various advances in science and medicine.

The nature of the family will change. Due to the ever increasing lifespan, there will be more and more second and third marriages, many more step-siblings, half-siblings and step-grandchildren, etc.

Doctors will be kept busy with face lifts, tucks, transplants, etc. as people continually expect to look as young as they feel.

Even now, Club Houses are equipped with the best Nautilus exercise equipment. They offer massage therapy, saunas, jacuzzi, indoor swimming pools, bars and restaurants.

Club Houses are becoming 24 hour night clubs. They will serve liquor, have more live entertainment and offer the residents more and more amenities.

As time goes on, residents will be able to shop by phone line, television and computer hook-up and never have to leave the community. Homes will be self cleaning and fully computerized.

I can envision a time when mature models will be walking down runways, modeling the latest fashions for mature women. Real clothes. Attractive clothes. Clothes that bring out the real beauty in the mature woman.

Chapter Fifteen
Some Do's and Some Don'ts

When you're considering retirement and a move to an active adult community, there are a number of do's and don'ts which you should consider.

By all means do look for:
snow removal
cutting of the grass
garbage pick up
age—you want a young community

Is there a brisk walking trail—this is very important. Few activities are as beneficial and easy to participate as walking.

Do the homes have fireplaces? This is a nice touch as are optional sunrooms and television rooms. Of course, you want plenty of closet space and large bedrooms.

Find out an estimate of the property and utility taxes. Although they should not be nearly so burdensome as owning your old home, you should have a clear idea of what your expenses will be.

Find out the background of the builder of the community. You have lived long enough not to enter into such an important decision with blinders on.

You should know the recreational facilities provided to residents and which community services are covered by your monthly fee. Is the community cable ready? Does it have Bocci courts? Shuffleboard courts? At least four tennis courts?

You want 24 hour security service—make sure you have it. You should also expect to have a full time activities director. Look for hardwood floors in the Main Entertainment room. Gas heat. Music system in the Club House and around the pool. A stage.

Simple attention to detail will make your life so much more pleasant. Does the kitchen have a microwave? Are there curved corners in the kitchen? Self-cleaning ovens?

Is there air conditioning in the home? Is there vinyl siding on the exterior of the house? A two car garage? Individual mailboxes at the curbside? Is the house energy efficient? Does it have insulated, double-paned glass windows? A forty-gallon hot water heater?

You definitely don't want to have high ceilings. Although they are attractive, they are not energy efficient and they are difficult to clean.

You do not want a community with to many rules. Obviously, you do want some rules. For example, the hours when grandchildren can use the swimming pool, when the Club House closes, no smoking in the Club House. However, too many rules become cumbersome.

Also, don't upgrade too much. You want your home to be warm and comfortable. You are in a new and wonderful stage of your life. Take it from me, I've seen this over and over—you'll be so busy that you'll be out of you house most of the time. Keep the extra money for a nest egg, for traveling or for buying your honey something special. Go with the standard home. If you pick out a vanilla color for the bathroom, you can always highlight it with accessories.

Don't—let me repeat, DON'T—give everything away. Never, never, never get rid of your valuables or your possessions. Some people seem to think they won't be needing them once they live in an adult community. Why on earth not?

China, silver, crystal—even sewing machines and bowling balls. Gentlemen, your electric saws. If you're a handyman and you enjoy working with your tools, keep them! If you are a lady who enjoys entertaining, keep your beautiful tablecloths and napkins. You'll still be entertaining. You'll be meeting new friends and will be proud of your new home.

Men, you'll finally have the time to enjoy puttering in the garage instead of feeling burdened and badgered by the chores.

This is a transition in life, not a dramatic change. Don't throw your past away, just embrace your future!

Of course, the biggest "don't" is: Don't be afraid to move into an active adult community. It will be the best move you ever make. You will never again be alone or afraid. You will be surrounded by people who care about you and who share your interests and problems. You're all in the same boat, so to speak. You're going through the same changes and have the same reactions to those changes.

If you happen to be single, this advice goes double for you! It gives you the chance to have a wonderful, active lifestyle without the awkwardness of being the "third spoke." More and more singles are moving into active adult communities—if only for the security.

Whatever you do, don't stay in that big house on that quiet street just staring out the window everyday. Get out there and visit an adult community. See for yourself what your future could hold for you!

Chapter Sixteen
A Simple Recipe

So often I am asked for a "recipe" for a successful and active adult lifestyle. Well, I finally decided to jot it down and here it is:

15 cups of wonderful people
13 cups of smiles
18 cups of laughter
1 oz. of sitting
20 cups of relaxation
200 cups of activities
50 cups of exercise
1 peck of sleeping
100 cups of fun
50 cups of love
1/2 peck of work
25 cups of sharing
18 cups of caring
150 cups of parties

Mix the above ingredients thoroughly with a spoon, joyously.

If you can relate to this lifestyle, then hurry and cut yourself a slice of the pie—before it's all gone!

Chapter Seventeen
Looking For Love in the Right Places...

There are Singles clubs popping up in all adult communities. The best change I see in this is that the singles clubs are beginning to separate themselves from the married couples. They have begun to have their own "New York Parties," dances and trips.

I think this is very healthy. In the past, as supportive as the entire community has been to everyone else, the reality is that the needs of the single active adult are different than the needs of the married adult. It can be awkward for singles to be around married couples all the time.

Hey, they are single and proud of it. They want to meet other single people.

There should be a singles club for mature adults all over the world. I've seen residents meet and fall in love during Arts and Crafts. I've seen them meet when they were bowling on the same bowling team.

One couple met and fell in love when Barbara was on the pool badge committee. Don needed a badge and... well, as they say, the rest is history. He fell in love with Barbara as soon as he laid eyes on her.

Yes, they got married. Now they're having a wonderful time with the married couples. (They still spend a lot of time with their single friends too!)

However, marriage is a very big decision for mature adults. There are so many securities that they would lose. Sometimes, they choose to be in love and be together, but they keep their securities.

This is another fact that has to be looked at "head on." We have created a situation where people are penalized for falling in love and getting married. That is not right.

Mature adult communities should work hard to satisfy the needs of the residents. In big and small ways. How many times have mature adults complained to grocery store managers that food is shelved either too high or too low for them? And often the labels of the shelves are printed in letters too small for adults to read.

Adult communities should have food stores for their residents, stores that cater to their needs, their food choices—and their physical convenience.

Likewise, every adult community should have a fully equipped exercise room with a complete Nautilus set-up. There should be a trainer available by appointment because it is very important that every person have an exercise routine tailored to his or her needs. Otherwise, it is possible to do more damage than good.

The goal of exercise is to get in shape, stay in

shape, feel stronger and healthier. The trainer will make sure that the equipment is used properly to that end. You will be surprised how much better you will feel in just a few short weeks of a supervised and personal program.

Exercise is a must. To be happily active you have to get that machine, your body, working efficiently and effectively. Get into an exercise program right away—even before you finish unpacking your cartons and boxes. You will be glad you did!

One of the nicest things about working with active adults is seeing the change in them after only a couple of months in the community. They seem to develop an appetite for living, a lust for life that is genuinely rewarding to see.

And it is all because of their new lifestyle. Busy, busy, busy!

They feel that they; are in the flow of things again. The same feeling they had when their first child was born—all consuming and all rewarding.

Remember how that was? Every aspect of that baby was precious and uplifting. The same is true in terms of the changes in the active adult community. Every change, large and small, seems to be uplifting and rewarding. It is exciting and it makes clear that there is so much to look forward to, so much to live for.

Moving into an active adult community will

add ten years to your life. Ten years of real living, of fun, activity, enjoyment, of friends, family and sharing.

That is what this new lifestyle can do.

Chapter Eighteen
Let's Talk Lifestyle

The most important thing about a new lifestyle is that it be one that you can take advantage of. If you are in a difficult place psychologically then you need to get to a better place.

The single best piece of advice I can give anyone is to SMILE! But if you are depressed then you need to find happy things to do to help you get out of your blue mood.

1. Buy your grandson or granddaughter a toy. The happiness on their faces will light up your heart.

2. Take a long walk.

3. Take a bike ride.

4. Call a friend.

5. Take in a funny movie.

6. If you live close to a lake or the ocean—just sit and watch the water.

7. Take a walk on the boardwalk.

8. Make popcorn.

9. Make homemade bread.

10. Eat a candy bar.

11. Rent the video, "Casablanca" or a good John Wayne western.

12. Bake cookies.

13. Write a love note to your mate.

14. Put a log on the fire.

15. Visit a shut-in.

16. Get a massage.

17. Swing in a hammock.

18. Take a ride in a boat.

19. Take a ride on a wave-runner.

20. Get a new hair-do.

21. Meet a new friend.

22. Get involved in a project of some kind. Models. Puzzles. Crosswords.

23. Play your favorite song on your stereo.

24. Take a day trip.

25. Go fishing or crabbing.

26. Tell a funny joke.

27. Laugh, laugh, laugh.

Do you really think we are here forever? Of course not! This is our life and we have to make the best of it. With that in mind, let's talk lifestyle. Let's learn about people who have turned their lives around.

The lifestyle you should expect in an adult community is one where the residents are enthusiastic about life in general. They want to try new experiences, they want to learn new sports, go to new places, enjoy dinners and lunch together.

They celebrate every holiday—and celebrate a lot of non-holidays too! The feeling they create is one in which everyone is secure and never alone. It's sharing your life with fun and wonderful people.

Many singles—especially women—are moving into active adult communities. They are finding a wonderful life of activities and interesting people in a safe and secure environment. Retirement communities are not just for married couples. Single men and women live there and love being there.

Because people are retiring at ever-younger ages, the people living in retirement communities are getting younger and younger. This adds to the level of activity and fun. Everyone should "take the bull by the horns" and embrace a new, fuller lifestyle, one which will allow them to get the most out of this next stage in their lives!

Chapter Nineteen
Meet New Friends

"I feel young again."

This is how Mary explained the flowers in her hand. "I guess you can tell that Bob and I are still madly in love," she said, glancing down at the flowers. They'd been married 20 months earlier. At 68, Mary laughed about her age difference with Bob. "He's only 60. People tease me about robbing the cradle, but we just laugh along with them."

"Bob said he fell in love with me because of my zest for life. He was married twice before, both times to younger women and they both cheated on him. I guess he's decided that older is the way to go," she added with a smile.

"That's not it," Bob said. "Mary is a beautiful woman," he said to me. "Look at those blue eyes. And not a wrinkle on her face. Her hair is still gorgeous. When she told me how old she was I almost fell out of my chair. She could be a model."

They decided to move to Florida together and start their lives over.

"We've been given a second chance and we plan on taking it with all the gusto we've got!" Mary said. "Our children didn't come to the wedding.

They think we're being silly. "Why get married?," they wanted to know. Bob's children think I'm too old for him."

"Sure, I'd prefer that they were happy for us, but what's important to me is that Bob loves me. Personally, I think his children think I'm marrying their father for his money. That's ridiculous. They should be happy for him. He's not alone. And neither am I!"

"Life goes by like pages in a book," Bob agreed. "If you don't try to enjoy some of it, it's too late. It's gone."

"We're happy together. That's what's important. We're happy. I hope someday our families will become one, but we can't control that. We're just lucky we found each other."

I could see by the glow in his eyes that he meant every word. And the way Mary held to his arm told me that she felt the same way. They were happy as two people could be. I thought it was sad that their children didn't come to their wedding.

Just then, a voice rang out, "Dad! Dad!"

Bob looked up. A young man was walking quickly toward him. The look of astonishment and joy on Bob's face was priceless. Both he and Mary began to cry with happiness. Soon, everyone around them was crying.

"Dad, I'm happy for you both. I grew up

overnight! I just love you, Dad. That's all."
"I know you do, son," Bob said, struggling to find his voice. "Now, give Mary a kiss, would you?"

He did and then, behind him, all the rest of the family joined in welcoming Mary into "the fold."

So, the circle of life goes on and on. Sure, sometimes it's difficult, but love finds a way —even when you've "robbed the cradle!"

Ann was born in Ohio. She married when she was 18 and remained married for 40 years. During those years, she gave birth to and raised four children while her husband struggled through a series of jobs—milk man, security guard. Then Bill got sick and had a heart attack. He died shortly after, leaving Ann alone. She thought her life was over until she began doing charity work at local hospitals. She met a woman, Marion, whom she became friendly with. They started going to dinners and the movies. Spent time together.

That changed when Marion met a man who lived down the street from her.

"She fell in love with him," Ann said. "I'll tell you, I thought they were the silliest fools I'd ever met, the way they were behaving. But then I realized that Marion was really happy and I wanted to be that happy too."

Ann decided to move to where there were more people her own age. Although she didn't marry again, she did meet a wonderful, sensitive man,

Frank. They've been going out for three years. It almost embarrasses Ann to admit how happy she is.

"Anyone who lives alone should get out of the house," she says. "Get involved. Get busy and find yourself a soul mate. You know," she added in a whisper, "my sex life is great now too!"

"I stuck with her because that's what you did then," Phil said of his first wife of 35 years. He'd dreamed of being a professional baseball player, but getting married and having children effectively put an end to that dream. He worked and supported Gladys and the children. When the children were grown though, he decided that he couldn't remain in the marriage and divorced.

"I think it's harder for men to be alone than it is for women," he said. "Women find things to do around the house, but men hate it. Women love to talk on the phone, but men hate it."

"I knew I would have to get involved with something. At the time, I was still working as a management consultant. A co-worker told me about a Democratic meeting so I went. Glad I did. I found the most beautiful Irish girl there, Kate."

"She was so full of life, cooking, shopping or travelling to see one of her four children. Kate told me to get with it, life wasn't forever and jump on the train before it's too late!"

"I was at her house every night, watching the news. She told me to sell my house and move in with her. I'd just laugh and tell her to sell her house and come and clean mine! She said, No way! "Look, I know what love really is. It's sharing a cup of coffee, eating something you shouldn't together, hoping your children don't find out."

"I only have one life here and I'm living it the way I want to was her attitude. It was funny. I didn't think I would ever talk like that. I just didn't talk about my personal life. But what the hell? I thought. Who really cares? I mean, I'm telling you this story, right?"

"I just want to help anyone who's dating a person who makes you feel good or happy. Enjoy being with him or her. Don't waste time. Like Kate said, Life isn't forever."

"Well, my Katie's heart did finally give out last year and I never had the chance to tell her how I really felt. If Kate could hear this, I want her to know that she was the joy of my life. She was my reason to get out of bed in the morning. She was the song in my heart. My sun in the day. My moon in the night. She gave me feelings I never had with anyone. I loved her with all my heart and I will miss her. Forever."

What too many people fail to understand about becoming an active adult is that is is often the beginning of a wonderful stage, one that can fire the senses and the emotions as much as—or more—than any other time in our lives.

Chapter Twenty
What's Age Got To Do With It?

How does that joke go? What's the definition of an optimist? An 85 year old man who gets married and then shops for a new house—near a school!

Friends, it's time we all stop laughing and take our blinders off! Love is the most powerful of human emotions and sexuality is an integral part of any loving relationship. For too long, we've labored under the false illusion that folks after "a certain age" are no longer interested in love and sex.

Wrong!

It wasn't long ago that I met a man in his late 30s who expressed some confusion regarding a new relationship his mother was in.

"I don't get it," he admitted freely. "She has grandchildren..."

"So?" I asked.

"So, isn't that enough?"

"Grandchildren are wonderful," I told him. "And I'm sure your mother adores her grandchildren. But you didn't really expect her to sit around and knit sweaters for the rest of her life, did you?"

"Well, I..."

He couldn't quite reconcile his image of his aging mother—the way his mother was "supposed to behave"—with the still vibrant woman who was planning a cruise to Alaska with "a man."

I didn't share with him what I knew about the planned trip to Alaska, that his mother and her new boyfriend were going to be sharing the same bedroom on the cruise.

We have all been victimized by the so-called youth culture in this country for too long. As a result, too often we are ready to put our senior citizens "out to pasture." But we'd best not be too hasty about putting anyone out to pasture unless there are some fields out there where they can sow their oats.

Life, my friends, is for living—from start to finish!

Chapter Twenty-One
Love in the Bowling Lane

The bowling alley was loud but it was sure a lot better than sitting alone in a living room and watching television. That's how Peg felt about it when she first joined the bowling league four months earlier. The first team she joined was an all-ladies team that had a wonderful time finishing fifth in a six-team league.

She became friendly with most of her teammates and found that she enjoyed their company in places other than the bowling alley. So, her teammates were a little surprised to learn that Peg wasn't going to rejoin their team for the next session.

"We need you, Peg," they said. "Who else can consistently bowl in the 90s?"

Peg laughed. "You're right, I'm quite a bowler, aren't I? But I'm not rejoining the team."

"Why not, Peg?"

"Because," she told them, "I've signed on for the men and women's league."

The ladies were stunned to silence. Such a

jump was almost unheard of after only one session. The mixed league was for "real players," not a bunch of ladies out just to have a good time.

"Are you sure?" they asked Peg.

Peg smiled. "No. That's why I'm doing it."

In spite of her bravado, Peg was nervous the first night of the mixed league. After all, she had sat in the back and watched this league more than once. Her new teammates seemed nice enough. There was Mary, a plump, cheerful woman of 68. Bill was tall and angular at 72. Ruth, at 67, was small and delicate, even smaller than Peg herself.

As Peg turned to choose the bowling ball she would use, she couldn't help but think how young they seemed. At 84, she was far and away the oldest member of the team.

She had been a widow for nearly17 years. During that time, she had devoted herself to her daughters and her grandchildren, to her church activities and to her volunteer work at the local hospital.

She loved all those things, but somehow something was missing. When her friend, Beth, suggested a bowling league, Peg had scoffed. "Bowling? The ball probably weighs as much as I do! Maybe more!"

"Come on, we'll give it a try. What harm could it do?"

Peg shrugged. None that she could think of. "What if I don't knock down any of the pins?"
Beth laughed. "Then we move on to miniature golf!"

Peg was happily surprised her first time out. Although the ball was heavy she didn't have any trouble rolling it down the smooth lane. She had more than her share of gutter balls, but she also knocked down 47 pins.

"Ya-hoo!" she said as she released the ball in the tenth frame.

"Ya-hoo?" Beth asked when Peg returned to her seat.

Peg laughed. "Sounded right to me."

Peg quickly came to feel right at home in the bowling league. Her daughters joked about their mother's new-found activity. "She's not really bowling," they joked to each other. "She's out chasing men."

"Maybe I am," Peg said slyly when she heard about their good-natured teasing.

"You're not!" was their response. But Peg didn't say anything to them.

Her first game on the mixed team was not impressive, but she found that she was having a good time and that her teammates were all glad to have her aboard. Before the tenth frame she was back to her comfortable, "Ya-hoo!" as she released the ball.

By the second night of the mixed league she was being referred to as "Ya-hoo!" by nearly everyone in the bowling alley. She kind of liked it.

During that second night, she was drying her hand on the drier at the end of the lane when she looked up and locked eyes with a gentleman bowling in another lane.

"Let's go, Ya-hoo!" her teammates called out, clapping their hands good-naturedly.

"Bowl me a strike!" Mary said.

Peg managed to break the eye contact and pick up her bowling ball. She rolled it down the lane without her familiar "Ya-hoo!" and managed only a gutter ball and three pins down. When she came back to her seat, she leaned over to Ruth and whispered, "Who's that gentleman over there?"

Ruth raised her head and looked in the direction Peg indicated. "The bald man with glasses?"

Peg shook her head. "No. The tall, slim one."

"Oh him," Ruth said with a smile. "That's Dave."

"Introduce me," Peg said with uncharacteristic urgency.

Ruth looked at her in surprise. "I..."

"Please"

A short time later, after several more frames of half-hearted "Ya-hoos," Peg was following Ruth toward the snack counter for a soft drink. As they did, Dave came toward them.

"Oh Lord," Peg thought. "He's coming this way."

"Hello, Dave," Ruth said, smiling sweetly.

"Hello, Ruth," he said, never taking his eyes off Peg.
"How are you?"

"Dave, this is my good friend..."

"Ya-hoo," Dave said, extending his hand to Peg. "A pleasure to meet you."

Peg took his hand. His grasp was warm and comforting. She realized that she hadn't felt such a grasp in a long, long time.

They shared a soft drink that first night, sitting side by side on the stools at the snack counter. They talked about a great many things—grandchildren, television programs, friends, things they'd always wanted to do—and they discovered they had a great deal in common.

"When I saw him," Peg later explained to Ruth, "it was so clear to me. He was the one."

Ruth's eyes twinkled and she smiled with genuine pleasure.

Peg and Dave became a fixture at the bowling alley, always together, holding hands, stealing kisses.

"Like newlyweds," someone observed one evening.

Which is what they were a few short months later. Both 85 years young, they began house hunting and shopping around for furniture.

"We're going to Hawaii for our honeymoon," Peg explained to her teammates.

There were a number of winks and nods and then Ruth sidled up to Peg and whispered, "Better be careful. You might get pregnant."

"Oh no, I can't," Peg replied honestly. "I'm on the pill."

And so it goes. So it goes.

Chapter Twenty-two
Being Alone Can be Positive

I am a full-time director of resident activities at an active adult community dedicated to the needs of mature adults. In this capacity I have met with a wide range of adults who have arrived at a point in their lives when they are free of so many of the burdens that make life difficult. When I tell you that the best times are yet to come, I know what I'm saying.

People retiring today are starting an entirely new phase in their lives. Upcoming are many healthy, active years ahead. Folks of these age groups are looking forward to developing new ideas about how to spend all that free time.

After years of hard work, raising a family and dedicating themselves to everyone else, it can be a strange and difficult switch to concentrate on their own needs and wishes.

Believe me though, it's only hard in the beginning...

Peg and Dave's experience is wonderful, but I have found that there is a great deal of variety among the people I have spoken to in how they have turned their later years into the most fulfilling of their lives. And, as I have discovered, finding a new partner is not always the solution. Sometimes it is simply finding oneself.

Carol is a perfect example of an older woman who decided that "enough was enough." She had been married to Bill for over 40 years, years which she has described as being terribly unhappy.

"They say that we become like our parents. Well, I didn't want that to happen," Carol admitted freely. "My mom and dad were married in an unhappy marriage for nearly 50 years."

"Maybe it was the Catholic upbringing that kept them together. It might have kept them together, but it sure didn't keep them happy—with themselves or with each other."

"I didn't realize until my own children told me that I should leave my husband that I was just like my mother." Carol shook her head. "My parents' marriage ended when my father died. 'Til death do us part, I guess. Mom never did marry again."

"I never had much of a life and I sure never had a model for what a marriage *should* or *could* be."

Carol's husband was very domineering, insisting on taking care of all the finances for the family. He kept all the money and he paid the bills, giving Carol a small "allowance" so she could take care of household needs. As a result, she viewed being alone as being a frightening experience.

"I didn't feel I had the tools," she said. But her unhappiness and the urging of her children finally turned the tide. She got a divorce and suddenly, a whole new life opened up to her.

"No, I couldn't say it was easy. Not at first anyway. And there are still times when things are tough. Like when my car breaks down or the plumbing goes. Life's little pleasures," she added with a smile. "But I manage and each time I get through one difficulty I feel stronger to face the next one."

"In spite of the difficulties, I can't believe how free I feel. I'm making new friends now—making friends was always difficult when I was married —and I'm doing things I'd only dreamed of doing before."

"Do you know, I'm planning on joining a bicycle tour of New England this summer?" She laughed. "When I was married doing something like that would have been as likely as being an astronaut."

Carol has made a new life for herself, a successful and fulfilling life. It wasn't money that has turned her new life into something closer to her dreams. It wasn't luck—over 40 years in a bad marriage isn't the best of luck. What has made Carol's life so much better is her determination to *remain active*.

"New memories" should be the goal of active adults, new memories to be enjoyed along with old memories.

Carol decided to "break free" from a life she no longer valued. Unfortunately, many adults come to find themselves alone by anything but design.

I cannot tell you how many times I have sat down with lovely, lovely people who find themselves lost in the world because they have lost the people they had been closest to.

"We had planned for these years together and now I'm alone..." is a refrain I have heard often. There is no way to minimize the trauma that losing one's life partner causes. Each of us must mourn that loss in our own way. However, there comes a time when we all must understand that our lives are for living. Our memories are to be cherished, but that we must go on.

Sometimes "going on" demands that we move along more than psychologically, but also physically. This was the case with Marjorie, a woman that I came to know only a short while ago.

She had moved up from Florida not long after her husband passed away.

"I couldn't bear to stay there," she said to me as we walked along a tree-lined path. "I just couldn't stand the memories. Charles and I had been going down to Florida for the past ten or 15 years. Only five years ago we decided to buy a condominium and live there year round."

"We thought of it as our own little paradise. But," she went on, pausing on our walk and looking me in the eye, "paradise didn't seem so wonderful anymore."

I nodded my head, understanding.

"Charlie and I had a beautiful life together. He was my best friend." She smiled a quick, thoughtful smile. "It's funny. You think you'll be together forever and ever and then, just like that, it's over."

"It used to be my neighbor or a friend. Always someone else. Then, one day it was Charles. It was all so fast. He went for a check-up on a Monday last September and bang, the doctor said there was nothing he could do for him."

"He couldn't believe his ears. He hadn't felt bad. A little tired maybe, but nothing to make him concerned. But the doctor said there was nothing to be done. He said Charles should go home and enjoy the rest of his life."

"It was the cancer of course. It had spread throughout his body. The doctor couldn't understand why Charles hadn't suffered from more symptoms."

"He wasn't an old man. Not old at all. Just three years older than me. Now I'm 72 years young and I'm alone. I came back up to the northeast because that's where my children are. It's important for me to be close to family."

Marjorie and I talked many times over the next few weeks. Although she loved her children and their families and needed to be close to them, she was equally determined not to become a burden to them. She also wanted to enjoy her life. She and Charles had always been so active and happy.

"Charles wouldn't want me to be sad," she said to me one day.

Marjorie decided to move into an active adult community. The decision was one of the best she'd ever made. "I'm still alone," she told me recently. "There's nothing I can do about my Charles being gone. I miss him still. But it makes a big difference being around so many wonderful people."

"Everyone here really cares about one another. Just last night, my next door neighbor came over and asked me to go to dinner with her and her husband."

"I'm able to socialize here. There are games and classes and interesting people. And we have 24 hour security. It is a Godsend to feel protected from the things that plague others in society."

"And I like my independence. I see my family a lot. They come and see me here or I visit them."

"If I have to live a life without Charles then I would have to say that this is as close to paradise as I can imagine getting."

Jake understands what it's like to feel alone.

"I've had a lot of time to be alone," he explained. "I was married when I was young for ten years. we never had any children, so I'm pretty much by myself now."

"I'll tell you, life can get lonely if you don't make sure you're around people. The television's okay, but it can't take the place of real people doing real things."

Jake loves living in an active adult community because of the sense of community it affords him. He continues to work part-time as a financial consultant.

"First thing I do when I get home is get washed up and then head for the club house," he says. "I like to work out—oh, nothing like I did when I was a kid, but the doctors all say that exercise is the key to staying healthy. I like to exercise.

"We have a lady who comes in four days a week to lead exercise classes. There's also a young man who is here everyday to help out with weight exercises.

I can't lift as much as I did when I was younger, but I think I look pretty good for a guy my age. More to the point, I *feel* good."

"There are other times when I'll be reading and I'll get to feel a bit lonely. I'll put my book down and head on over to the Club House. There's always a group of guys there, playing cards or shooting a little pool. Penny ante stuff, but a lot of fun."

"We're not there for the cards, but for the companionship. We watch out for each other. If someone doesn't show up a couple of evenings we call and visit—just to make sure everything's all right."

"I'd say that we all think of ourselves as being in one big family here. I like that."

"If anyone was to ask me what I thought about being in an active adult community, I'd tell them that it was the best thing I ever did. I wish I could have been here when I was younger."

"I have friends, activities, places to go. I don't have to worry about driving anyplace because everything's within walking distance."

"I wouldn't give this up for anything. No, if anyone asked me I'd tell them that living in an active adult community is the best thing they could do for themselves. Heck, if I hit the lottery tomorrow I wouldn't move. I couldn't be happier than I am now. No way."

Chapter Twenty-three
Recreation

"Last one in the pool's a rotten egg!"

Sound like a pool party for teenagers? Well, to talk to my friends it sounds like another fun day in the sun by the pool. Or, put another way, Youth is wasted on the Young!

Oh sure, we have dispensed with most of the silliness of those long ago years, but that doesn't mean that we don't know how to have fun. Just the other day, we enjoyed a "Pool Fashion and Barbeque" party. Not only was it a wonderful opportunity for the newer residents of the community to get to know the other residents, it was also a great chance to take advantage of the beautiful day.

Even though we are constantly told that ours is a "youth culture" more and more people are coming to recognize the growing community of active adults in the United States. Was it only a generation ago that we were expected to wear only drab colors and look miserable as we matured?

Thankfully that time is gone!

At our pool party a full line of colorful adult wear was displayed—and modeled! Even some of our long time residents were surprised to see just how the clothing industry has caught up with the active lifestyle of the more mature adult. The clothes were bright and colorful and, more to the point, comfortable and easy to wear. They were designed with a full range of activities in mind.

"There should be a magazine that advertises these things," Betty commented to me.

"Who needs a magazine—they're here for us!" her friend, Sheila, said.

In addition to the fashion show there was a scrumptious barbeque of hamburgers, hot dogs, chicken, corn on the cob, all kinds of salads and fresh fruits. Live music played at pool side as residents ate, joked, danced a little and yes, swam.

During the summer months, the pool and the patio are a focal point of the community with water aerobics offered three times during the day, open swimming, lap swimming along with cards, mah jong, and other table games in the fresh air.

"I love the pool," Joe, a five-year resident crowed. "It's great for my back."

While exercise "fads" tend to come and go, swimming for fitness and improved health are always a good idea—especially for active adults.

Unlike some other exercises, swimming has a minimal risk of injury. There is almost no stress placed on bones and joints, making it a wonderful form of cardiovascular exercise.

The reason that such a "strenuous" activity is so easy on the body is simple—the water supports your weight. As we all begin to realize at some point in our lives, gravity is not always our friend. Oh sure, it keeps us rooted right here on mother earth, but it also makes our backs ache, our muscles sag, our ankles swell... you know the litany. Swimming, because we are all buoyant in the water, is an exercise that minimizes the burdens of gravity.

Because swimming is a fluid exercise (no pun intended!) there is minimal stress on internal organs. Joggers know all about the stress that can result from high impact activities.

A vigorous swim is wonderful for the heart and for the major muscle groups in the body. In addition, it puts many joints through a full range of motion.

"But I was never much of a swimmer," complained one of our residents when I explained the benefits of swimming to him.

"That's all right. You don't need to become an Olympic swimmer. But you do have to do a little bit of work to get all the benefits of swimming. If you just swim hard enough three or four times a week to feel pleasantly tired the next day you can be sure you're getting the benefits of swimming."

The line between recreation and exercise is a fine one. No one should overdo it the first few times out. Swim moderately the first times out and then see how you react.

One word of caution—because blood pressure falls when you are in a pool (another side effect of buoyancy) there is a slight chance of feeling "woozy" or even passing out when you come out from the water, especially if you take hypertension drugs. If that happens, it is important to check in with your doctor.

Other than that, swimming is a wonderful exercise and a fun activity in the community.

On any given weekend, there are also younger people visiting—grandchildren and other family members of residents. Inevitably, they are all well-behaved. The residents impress upon them the need to have respect for the residents and to behave appropriately.

When someone calls out, "Last one in the pool...!", young visitors understand that the call is not necessarily for them!

Often, people will ask me about the activities available for active adults. They immediately think that golf is the most demanding recreational activity that we offer. I am always happy to set them to rights.

"Of course there is golf and many of our residents will golf a full 18 holes three to four times a week. However, golf is just one of the many activities available to our residents. We also have tennis facilities, horse shoes, boccie ball, shuffleboard and exercise classes."

"Our residents not only participate in all of these scheduled activities, most of which have instructors throughout the day, but they also take advantage of our nature trails for brisk walking and our bicycle paths. We really believe it when we say *active* adult!"

Chapter Twenty-four
Some Questions

Retirement is such a momentous point in our lives. With that decision to stop working, we change directions from a path that we have been on for our entire adult lives. Even though many people plan for their retirement, they find that retired life is not what they expected.

When they begin to look at an active adult community, they have many questions. Some of the questions are the result of inbred resistance. Many people feel that they should live in the same house they've been living in for their adult lives, at least as long as they are able.

Ron and Vera had no trouble leaving their house though.

"Leaving our home of 28 years was the easy part," Vera confessed. "We had really had enough of all the work that a big house involves. We wanted to spend time with each other—not take care of a house."

"No, the decision to leave our home was easy. It was finding a house to move into that was hard."

Ron and Vera looked first in their community, hoping to simply "down-size" their house. They looked at condominiums and apartments, but found them to be too cramped.

"We wanted something special," Ron said. "We weren't leaving our house because we had to. We were leaving because we wanted to."

"Hey, I am 66 years old, but I don't think of myself as being old. I'm healthy and happy. Sometimes I look in the mirror and I'm surprised to see gray hair. Inside, I still feel like the 35 or 40 year old I was a quarter of a century or so ago."

A fundamental change occurred in the way retirement aged people viewed themselves. Although they are physically somewhere between 55 and 65 and up, their lifestyles do not change dramatically.

Most remain active even though some of their activities change. Most have the mental attitude of a person ten to 15 years younger, in spite of their chronological age.

Because most people entering this age group don't think of themselves as belonging to an age group that should be considering retiring, their questions often revolve around the need to get comfortable with what is awaiting them in an active adult community.

One of the first questions I am asked by potential residents is, "What kind of lifestyle should I expect?"

My answer is that they should expect a

lifestyle based on an enthusiasm about life in general.

"You mean, the people there are active and happy?"

Depending on how our conversation had been going, this question will often make me laugh.

"Of course," I tell them. "People retiring today are just like you—starting a new phase of their lives. There are many healthy, active years ahead. No one that I work with and meet is ready to throw in any towels yet.

"There are things to learn, ideas to develop, activities to enjoy..."

"You make it sound so wonderful."

"It is. Sure, it's sometimes tricky in the beginning, getting used to having all these wonderful things to do instead of going to work, but I've yet to meet a person who hasn't gotten used to it pretty quick."

"Our residents are learning new sports, arts and crafts, games—you name it. We're serious when we say 'active' adult. We'll show movies in the clubhouse, but we shy away from passive entertainment. Our residents want to do things and we want to help them."

"Our residents have the time to enjoy all these things now, time they didn't before. Before, they were working to pay the bills. Now they have the time to travel, go to dinners and lunches together."

"We have parties for every holiday and a few parties when there's no holiday at all."

"Our community is about feeling secure and never having to be alone. It's about sharing your life with wonderful, fun people."

The "common" view of adult communities is often reflected in the second most popular question I am asked, Do the lights go out early?

Of course, this is just a "nice way of asking, How boring is "retirement" life? Well, five years ago I might have had to say that, yes, it does get a little quiet in the evenings. But not today! People retiring in the 90s are very tuned into life. For them, retirement isn't a time to rest, but it's a time of greater freedom to DO, to do all the things they enjoy doing.

Almost every evening there are parties and card games. Movies are shown in the clubhouse. Pizza parties are held for a fun night. Even the mornings are fun. Residents have planned special breakfasts and not only are the residents all cooking the breakfasts themselves, all the cooks are men!

That alone should tell you that retirement today is a completely new and different time of life, a time of life to look forward to!

Okay, goes the next question, if it isn't "lights

out" at six o'clock, what time does the clubhouse close? I work in a very special active adult community.

This adult community has learned to listen to retired people to learn what they want, residents are given their own keys to the clubhouse. This translated into greater freedom.

For example, if a resident has guests from out of town at 11:00 at night and they want to play pool there's no problem at all. They can use the facility at any time they want.

When I say we like to emphasize the *active* in active adults I should hasten to add that we also respect the *adult* part of the term as well. Adults do not appreciate too many rules that limit their freedom. Adult communities are a lot like E.F. Hutton in that they listen!

We want our residents to take full advantage of their free time—whenever it is!

Although there has been a sea of change in terms of how mature adults behave—and are expected to behave—there is one thing that has remained constant, the absolute love of family. Although many grandparents are as likely to be found on a cruise as on a shuffleboard court, they all love their grandchildren and one of their big concerns in looking for an active adult community is how welcome their grandchildren will be when they come to visit.

The answer is, VERY WELCOME. Not only will they be welcomed they'll probably not want to leave at the end of their visit. There's as much for them to do as there is for you. There's boccie ball, shuffleboard, horseshoes, tennis, swimming, games... just to name a few things.

I've overheard more than one grandchild ask his grandmother if he could stay another week... please! You should see the pride and joy in their grandmother's faces when that happens.

Chapter 25
Giving the Old Business the Old Heave Ho!

Tony and Marie ran a small stationary store for nearly 35 years

"Every day it was the same thing," Marie said. "There were deliveries to worry about, greeting cards to unpack, papers, pens... everything."

"Not that there weren't a lot of pluses," Tony piped in. "We enjoyed a perfectly lovely life for those years. Not one year went by when we didn't make a nice profit. Not one."

"We worked hard for every penny," Marie reminded him with a knowing smile.

"Yes, we did," Tony agreed. "But we always knew it was going to be hard work."

Marie laughed. "Of course, the kids always had all the school supplies they needed."

"Not to mention summer jobs when they got older." Tony looked at me and he was beaming with pride. "We were able to employ our three children and a lot of their friends too. That was a good feeling."

Listening to them, I could tell that their store had not only been a lot of hard work, but it had been an important part of their lives. The store had been something of a gathering place for people in the community.

"We were as close as we could be to a community bulletin board. People would come in and tell us what was happening with their families and then other people would come in and we'd share news of graduations, parts in plays, Little League teams, sicknesses and sad things too," Marie said. "When we said we were closing, there were a lot of people who came in just to say good-bye."

Tony nodded. "We got a lot of letters from kids who worked for us," he said

"Not that they're kids anymore," Marie said with a faraway voice. "They're like our own children—with children of their own." She shook her head. "The time just flies."

After all those years though, running the store became more stressful and less rewarding. After all, their own children had grown up, gone to college, gotten married and begun families of their own.

"Running your own business is a hard taskmaster," Tony said. "There's always something that needs to be done. If it isn't the paperwork then it's the plumbing in the bathroom or paint or something.

And one time, when the alarm went off, the

police called here at two thirty in the morning. I'll tell you the truth, I'm too old to be waking up at two thirty in the morning."

In spite of all the difficulties, closing the store was not an easy decision for them. It was frightening to face the future which was so different than their past and present.

"Every day, even Sunday when we were closed, I knew what I was going to be doing," Marie said. "I had paperwork, books to keep, orders to fill in. I felt like I did when the kids went off to school—at a loss.

Still, they knew that it was time.

"It was time that we enjoyed our time together. We had that freedom. We'd worked hard enough to give ourselves some level of financial security. I mean, I loved the store, but I didn't want to die there," Tony said. "I wanted to have a life when I was still young and strong enough to enjoy it."

So, when Marie was 68 and Tony was 73 they closed the door to the store for the last time. Selling their house was the next thing, but after the store, they found selling the house to be easy.

And now?

"Ah, we love our life now," Marie said, her warm smile obviously sincere. "We walk, we play golf. We watch movies..."

"I couldn't even tell you how much a ream of paper costs these days," Tony joked. "But I could tell you how much it cost in '58."

Marie waved him away with a good-natured laugh. "And tell me, Tony, do you really care what a ream of paper cost in 1958?"

Tony laughed. "I'm not sure I cared in 1958."

They both agreed that it was wonderful to have the time to enjoy the good life.

"I tell you," Tony said. "I take a hot shower in the morning and I feel like I'm 21 years old again."

Marie eyed him with amusement. "So? Why don't you take your hot shower at night then?" she asked.

Chapter Twenty-six
Finding a New Family

Not only has "old age" changed for us, the world has changed for our children and grandchildren as well. Not that long ago, families still lived in the same community. Parents could expect to be close to their children well into their later years.

No more.

Now you are as likely to have your children spread out from London to Paris as from Long Island to Jersey City. We really do live in a global village.

But e-mail is not enough when it comes to family. Faxes, overnight mail, even twice-a-year visits of a week can't make up for the need we all have to have a "family" around us.

"I thought kids were supposed to take care of their parents when they got older," a friend of mine once complained. "I took care of my parents. But I don't think my kids will be taking care of me."

Certainly not in the way we cared for our parents. Now, three siblings might be spread out over thousands of miles without one within 700 miles of their parents. In this kind of environment, we all have to build our own, new families.

This is precisely where an active adult community can be most important to its residents. Too often we are so wrapped up in our children that we find ourselves somewhat isolated when they go off in search of their own lives and destinies.

That was the feeling that Alice and Fred had.

"Heck," Fred told me, "it seems like only a few days ago that I was coaching Little League and being a leader in the Scouts. Now, my boys are so far away. And I'm one of the lucky ones," he added quickly. "I speak with each of my boys at least once a week. I have friends who feel lucky if they speak to their kids on birthdays and holidays."

"Still, with one of my boys in California and the other in North Carolina, we don't see them as much as we'd like to."

"We have nice pictures of our grandchildren," Alice said. "Gorgeous."

"And we go out to see them as much as we can. It's harder for them to come to us, of course. Still, it's not what I was thinking of. No, not what I was thinking of."

"It was especially hard for Fred," Alice said. "He's nearly nine years older than I am, so he retired before I did. He spent a lot of time in the house."

"It wasn't that bad..."

"Oh no?" Alice asked, arching her eyebrows. "I remember how you were when I'd come home from work. You were like a lonely puppy dog waiting for someone to come home."

Fred shrugged. "I guess that's true. I didn't have much to do. There weren't a lot of golf games and I found myself isolated in the house. My day didn't really begin until after Alice came home from work."

"That changed when I retired," Alice said. "But then we both faced the same problem together. We traveled a bit, but it was mostly to visit our children and their families."

"In no time at all, we found ourselves in a rut. Our boys kept making suggestions about where we should go and what we should do, but to us it only sounded like they were saying that we should cut down our visits to them."

"We were wrong about that," Fred said. "They just wanted us to be happy and to enjoy our retirement."

"And frankly, that didn't happen until after we came to the retirement community."

Fred nodded his agreement.

"We love it. We feel like we're always on vacation. We don't have to worry about the yard or maintenance. There are activities all year around..."

"I'll tell you the truth," Fred confided, "When we're away, we miss the community. I miss the dances every Saturday night and Alice misses seeing her best friend, Sally."

Alice chuckled. "That's right. Fred doesn't really like the noise and lights of Atlantic City, but I love it. So, when the Community organizes a trip to Atlantic City, Sally and I go. Big spenders, the two of us."

"You won last time, didn't you?" Fred said.

"Came back $16.30 richer than when I left," Alice boasted. "Mostly Sally and I enjoy the shows."

"Gives me a headache," Fred said. "I'm much happier staying here and having a game of billiards with some of my friends."

They both were glad that they were able to do what they wanted to do knowing that the other was happy.

"Of course, I don't like being away from Fred for more than the day or two we're in Atlantic City. You know what they say, absence makes the heart grow fonder."

Fred smiled and reached out for Alice's hand. "We're probably closer now than we've been any time since our honeymoon."

"We wouldn't give up living here for anything."

"Nope," Fred agreed. "It's like being with one, big happy family."

Chapter Twenty-seven
Nobody Said There Weren't Challenges

While our retirement years open up whole new vistas, there is no denying that along with advanced years come additional challenges and health problems. I have been working with older, active adults for many years and have found them to be resourceful, imaginative and wonderful. I know that many of the people I work with have lots of "baggage" that they carry with them into their older years.

I think of Trudy and Bill, a couple who married just over five years ago. Trudy is now 68 and Bill is almost 75.

Trudy has a daughter, 45 years old, from her first marriage, a marriage that came to an end when her husband died. Bill has five children ranging in age from 32 to 43.

To see the two of them together would warm anyone's heart. The are considerate of each other's needs and take the time to make each other's lives as happy as possible. They both understand the challenges and difficulties of getting on in years.

"I like to enjoy life," Bill said. "I've even been called romantic by more than one person. But I'm not a foolish romantic and my eyes aren't closed.

We're born into this world to move along through it. We all die. That's a fact. Plain and simple."

Bill has already undergone open heart surgery, an experience which he claims made him a better person. Trudy has cancer. Neither is ignorant of the fact that they might not get to enjoy a full lifetime together.

"None of us knows how much time they have," Bill claimed philosophically. "All we can do is make the best use of it as we can."

It was that philosophy that was behind their decision to purchase a beautiful home in an active adult community.

"If one or the other of us should die then we wanted the other to have a beautiful home and to be surrounded by wonderful, caring people. That is what this community means to us," Trudy said. "It's a promise to each other that we will always care."

Trudy and Bill are perfect examples of people who acknowledge the difficulties of being a more mature adult, but who recognize that they can fill their days with happiness.

Active adults do not sit around and wait for the inevitable. They find things to do which bring them happiness and pleasure.

However, there is no denying that a very big key to being happy is being healthy. That old saying, So long as you've got your health... has more than a little wisdom to it.

Chapter Twenty-eight
You Gotta Have Heart

The old ticker is a constant concern for older adults. And it should be! Studies indicate that more people die in the United States from heart attacks than from all other diseases combined. The actual number of people suffering heart attacks each year is close to one and one-half million. Of these, less than half survive and of those who do, many die within two years of a subsequent attack.

These are frightening numbers, especially to those of us looking to fully enjoy our retirement years.

Studies have indicated that there are several factors that contribute to these numbers. Namely—genetic factors, dietary factors and cultural factors. In almost every study, there has been a direct link between heart disease and heart attack and the level of cholesterol in a person's blood.

"I've quit smoking," one resident boasts, but then adds in a lower voice, "I hope it's not too late."

So too the resident who is now watching his fatty food intake.

"But what exactly is cholesterol?" another asks.

Although the residents in an active adult community are all self-sufficient in their own private homes, one of the important services that is provided is health and nutrition counseling.

As an individual who has worked with active adults for many years, my goal is simple—for you to have many, <u>many</u> years of active and enjoyable experiences.

Our counselors have given clinics on the kinds of lifestyle changes mature adults should make to increase their chances of long years of good health.

In regards to healthy hearts, everyone should know that elevated cholesterol levels can be prevented or reduced in most people. Just as the most important element in planning a vacation is knowledge, the most important element in preventing any long-term disease such as heart disease is knowledge.

Diet is important, but dieting to lose weight is not necessarily the wisest decision. The primary concern should be diet and nutrition. Not just losing weight.

"But why can some people eat fatty foods and have a low cholesterol level and I, who have always been careful about what I eat, have a high level?" one of the residents asked me recently.

A simple analogy is to sunburn. Some people can withstand high levels of exposure to the sun without getting sunburned, while others do little more than step out onto the balcony for a minute or two and they burn.

Restricting fat in one's diet will not lower blood cholesterol levels significantly if that is the only change one makes. Because a healthy heart is the result of several factors—genetic, lifestyle and diet—the combination of changes one makes to keep their heart healthy is very individual and unique.

The first, best thing any of us can do to maintain a healthy heart is to NOT smoke. If we do smoke, the best thing to do is to QUIT.

The goal is to stop smoking, lose some weight (if you're overweight) and make the kind of dietary and lifestyle changes which will allow you to live long and *hearty*!

Lower fats, cut out refined sugars and increase your consumption of fiber and you will reduce your chances of suffering heart disease. And don't put off the changes. It's never too late to take control of your good health.

Chapter Twenty-nine
Okay, You've Got My Attention. What's Cholesterol Anyway?

Although this book is not a "health" book, it is very important to the active adult life that I promote that you take care of yourself! In order to accomplish this, you need information—knowledge.

Living long and happy is not an accident any more than having been financially successful was an accident. It took planning, hard work, skill and intelligence. Your hard work.

Now that you are retiring or are retired you have to use those same tools and skills to keep busy, happy and healthy.

We all hear a great deal about "cholesterol" but for the most part, we aren't clear on what exactly it is. Sure, we know it's in the blood and it can cause heart disease—but how?

Cholesterol is a waxy substance that is found in all animal fats and in egg yolks (yes, *that's* why they say you have to cut down on eggs!). More than 80% of the cholesterol found in our bodies is manufactured in our livers and in the epithelial (the single layer) cells in our intestinal tracts.

"If we manufacture cholesterol in our bodies how can it be bad?"

It's not "bad." Certainly not exclusively bad. Only when there is an excess in your blood. We all need cholesterol. Vitamin D, sex hormones (we'll get to that in a later chapter!) and bile salts all come from cholesterol.

Without cholesterol, cell walls wouldn't form properly. Nerve fibers would be without necessary insulation. Our skin wouldn't be waterproof...

Cholesterol is vital to our well being. But, a "little bit is good, a lot is deadly." Cholesterol is a lipid or fat. Fats do not dissolve in water. As a result, they are not easily broken down in our bodies.

When there is too much cholesterol in our systems, the excess is often deposited in the blood vessels, forming deposits that contribute to heart disease and to strokes.

One way to lower cholesterol is diet.

Cholesterol is present only in products of animal origin. That is, animal fat or dairy products. When the label says, "Hydrogenated..." it means <u>saturated</u>. Stay clear! When it comes to diet, the real villain is saturated fats. Cutting down on dietary cholesterol has little impact on blood cholesterol levels. Varying the amount of saturated fat in the diet <u>does</u> have a direct and dramatic impact on blood cholesterol levels.

What does this mean? Well, it suggests that those warnings about eating eggs might not be all that "on target."

"I can't keep track of everything the 'experts' tell me about staying healthy," complained one of my friends.

I had to agree. Sometimes it *is* difficult to sort through the mass of information and warnings that we hear to know what is significant and what is not. However, over time we can begin to get a general sense of the way to go.

Clearly, fat and especially saturated fat, must be more restricted in our diets than is the norm in the United States.

Still, one has to be careful about overreacting. As my own grandfather once said, "Everything in moderation."

Anytime we are asked to veer to one extreme or the other, we can assume that we are venturing off the best possible path. We must strike a delicate balance of foods and substances.

As my grandfather's advice suggested, the problem is not the consumption of fat in the diet, it is the <u>over consumption</u> that is the problem. The goal of healthy living is to add years to your life and still maintain the lifestyle that defines *for you* the quality of your life.

If you love your hamburger for dinner then be sure to off-set those fat calories by having a breakfast of fresh fruit and oatmeal. There is no reason that you cannot splurge on a dessert or meal—so long as you otherwise maintain a healthy, low fat diet!

"What about margarine? I've been told that margarine is better than butter."

Generally speaking, margarine is no better than butter. Most margarines contain oils that have been hydrogenated—made to be saturated. Additionally, the oils have most likely been heated up to high temperatures during the processing of margarine—research indicates that heated oil causes more arteriosclerosis than unheated.

A good rule of thumb in evaluating whether the fat content is saturated or unsaturated is, if the fat is a solid at room temperature then the fat is mostly saturated.

"Then what should I do in preparing meals?"

The butter versus margarine conflict is a tough one. However, other oils do show benefits. When mixing oils in salad dressing, you might consider olive oil. The best course is to avoid oils and fats altogether.

1. Poach, bake, broil or steam foods when possible.
2. Cook with non-stick pans or with a vegetable spray such as "Pam."
3. Trim the skin off chicken and turkey before cooking it.

4. Substitute lean choices of meat whenever possible. For example, Canadian bacon has less than half the fat of regular bacon.
5. Simply decrease the amount of fats, oil or butter your recipes call for.
6. Add non-fat food to recipes when possible. For example, add beans to chili and oatmeal to meatloaf. Use skim milk rather than whole. If you cannot tolerate skim, use 1%.
7. When you can see fat, such as on the edge of a beef steak, don't eat it. Trim it off with your knife and put it aside.
8. Substitute evaporated skimmed milk for cream.
9. Try fresh fruits and fresh fruit dishes for dessert instead of high fat pies, cakes and ice cream.
10. Avoid using fat filled condiments (ketchup, mayonnaise, etc.) unless they significantly enhance the flavor for you and then use them only sparingly.
11. Substitute low-fat mayonnaise for regular mayonnaise.
12. Use Neufchatel cheese instead of cream cheese.
13. Try non-fat yogurt in place of sour cream.
14. Make "cream" sauces from non-fat dry milk and arrowroot.
15. Instead of two eggs, use one yolk and two whites.

16. Experiment! Remove all the fat from your favorite recipes and see how they go. If no fat is successful, build them up from minimal fat contents until you have perfected them with minimum fat content.

Your retirement years have so much potential. Don't squander that potential by not taking care of yourself. Try and make the transition from high-fat to low-fat a fun transition.

If you are unhappy with a change in your diet or if you are forced to make drastic, unpleasant changes in tastes and lifestyle then the chances of maintaining those changes over the long term is not very good.

A healthy diet should be a life*long* experience! Your life is not a fad! Study labels! Cook from scratch when you can. Exercise control over your diet.

Control is the very thing we all want in our lives. Now that you have the freedom to live your life, make sure you don't jeopardize your freedom by making unwise choices.

Chapter Thirty
Now That I Understand Cholesterol, What's Fiber?

Like a juggler with one ball in the air—you're going to find that your "act" is incomplete until you can get something else going besides that one ball. In the case of a healthy diet, that means reducing fat *and* increasing fiber.

Like many terms thrown at us by the health/nutrition and medical professions, "fiber" seemed to explode on the scene, leaving us little time to understand just what the term referred to.

You have already probably begun increasing your fiber intake in cereals, breads (whole wheat, not white) and pastas. Still, whatever this "fiber" is, continues to escape you.

"Fiber" is the term used to denote substances derived from plants that are generally resistant to human digestive tract enzymes. That is, they don't get broken down in your stomach like most foods. Some of these fibers are soluble and insoluble. Both are important to your health.

A recent study indicated that certain insoluble fibers bind with bile acids and cholesterol, "carrying" the acids and cholesterol from the body. The soluble fibers are more useful in binding with water and increasing stool bulk and performing a laxative function.

Oat bran, dried beans and black-eyed peas are among the richest sources of fiber which can bind with and inhibit cholesterol. Of these, oat bran seems to be the best source for combating cholesterol.

You remember oat bran, responsible for that lovely, warm smelling concoction from long ago wintery mornings. It is easy on the digestive system and has the added benefit of modulating blood sugar levels—thereby preventing hunger. In other words, it "sticks to your ribs."

The average American diet contains about 20 grams of oat bran. Research suggests that the minimum amount should be over 30 grams daily and that doubling that quantity—to 60 grams—would be even more healthy.

Enjoy oatmeal or oatmeal muffins! Substitute oatmeal for hash browned potatoes, rice or even corn grits. Substitute oat bran for 1/3 of the flour called for in pancake or waffle recipes.

The retirement years are of adjustment and enjoyment. For many of us, they represent a complete change in lifestyle—from a working lifestyle to a leisure lifestyle. Certainly it would be wise to incorporate some of these simple nutritional changes into our changing lifestyles to help maintain good health.

Increase your high fiber foods, from fruits like apples, bananas, beets and carrots to oat bran, corn bran, peas and beans to green beans, cabbage, peanuts and tomatoes. This is not an extensive list.

All plants contain fiber in varying amounts. Fiber is a necessary structural component of plants. Because of this, each and every time you eat a food product derived from plants, you get some of the benefit of fiber consumption—provided the fiber has not been processed out of the food.

Here is a list of very simple changes you can make to increase the amount of dietary fiber you can get in your diet:

1. Leave the peels on apples when baking them or making applesauce.
2. Mix cooked beans into vegetable salads.
3. Develop recipes that contain black-eyed peas.
4. Add pinto beans and a little oat bran into chili.
5. Roll chicken in oat bran or corn bran before cooking.
6. Substitute half oat bran for flour in pan cake, waffle and crepe recipes.
7. Top low-fat yogurt with unpeeled peaches, apples or strawberries.
8. Make your own granola with rolled oats, oat bran, raisins, slivered almonds and dried fruit.
9. Juice oranges and grapefruit and use the pulp also.
10. Make tostadas with beans instead of beef.
11. Add corn bran, oat bran or rice bran to

vegetable soup.

12. Mix oat bran into beef patties for healthy hamburgers.

Make sure you are getting enough of the fiber you need in your diet.

1. Eat more than one serving of fiber-rich vegetables.
2. Eat a serving of leguminous food such as beans, peas or lentils.
3. Eat one or more servings of whole fruit such as apples, pears, citrus fruits or berries.
4. Eat foods containing oat bran such as oat bran itself, oatmeal muffins or other foods to which it has been added.

Let's eat well to stay healthy!

Chapter Thirty-one
No Contest, STOP Smoking

Believe me, I am not one to get preachy. I think that we must all be accepting of one another. I have come to appreciate that more and more as I get older. I also have come to appreciate that much more when I've had discussions with mature adults about all sorts of lifestyle issues (including sex, which is the next chapter!) But smoking is not just another choice. It is damaging to the smoker and everyone around him or her.

So, In spite of my determination not to preach, I will get up on my soapbox for this one because smoking not only shortens the number of days you have to enjoy on this earth, it also deprives you of the pleasures that you should be having while you're around.

If you are a smoker, you're probably used to being bombarded with messages—usually preachy messages—from friends and family about the evils of smoking. Painful as their words are, their advice is sound. As a smoker it is important to separate the "message from the messenger." While family and friends may be tedious or even rude with their advice, the content of their advice is good.

People who smoke a single pack of cigarettes a day increase their chances of suffering from lung cancer by 700%! The chances of suffering from other cancers is also increased—cancer of the larynx, 700%; cancer of the mouth, 900%; cancer of the esophagus, 300%; cancer of the pancreas, 170%. The risk of heart disease increases by 300%.

Increasing your consumption of cigarettes increases your risk. It is that simple.

What is sometimes overlooked by the general public in these anti-smoking statistics is that, statistically, smoking actually results in more deaths by heart attacks than from all forms of cancer. The common perception seems to focus on lung cancer, but statistics simply don't support that perception. Smoking attacks the heart! Your heart!

Your decision to begin smoking was based on a great many factors. As with all other aspects of your lifestyle, I only note them here to determine their impact on you cardiovascular health.

If you are a smoker who loves to smoke, the news is as bleak as an individual who enjoys French fries and lobster smothered in butter—your choices are damaging to your heart. Period.

You can dramatically reduce the risk of heart disease simply by quitting. Quitting is good for you!

A ten-year study observed a 21% reduction in the chance of heart disease among those who quit smoking. The Oslo study of dietary and smoking intervention in Norway revealed a statistically significant 47% reduction in heart attacks in the group of ex-smokers as compared to current smokers.

Dr. Lynn Rosenberg and associates assessed the effect of quitting smoking on the incidence of heart attack and reported their findings in the New England Journal of Medicine in 1985. Participating in the study were 1873 individuals who had a heart attack and 2775 who had not previously suffered any type of heart-disease related symptoms.

Among smokers who have been smoking for at least 20 years, the risk of cardiovascular disease is over four times that of non-smokers. However, those who smoke for at least 20 years and then quit almost eliminate any extra risk after two years of non-smoking.

Again, the message is, QUIT NOW!

The good news is that after non-smoking for two years, regardless of length of time smoking, the ex-smokers risk factor was reduced to almost that of the individual who never smoked.

Evidence suggests that any person, no matter how long they have been smoking can significantly reduce their chance of heart attack by stopping smoking permanently. That is good news.

However, if you're one of those smokers who have tried to quit, you know how difficult it is to stop. Why exactly is it so difficult to kick the habit?

A number of factors contribute to the difficulty, but they all come down to the same basic notion:

tobacco confers upon its users real benefits.

Recent studies suggest that tobacco use makes it easier to cope with overstimulation. This is because nicotine, a primary ingredient in tobacco, is a stimulus barrier, making it easier for a person to function in an environment that is overstimulating.

Nicotine *is* a drug and one of the primary reasons for the difficulty in breaking the cigarette habit is because cigarettes are addictive.

In fact, the Surgeon General of the United States has recently defined cigarette smokers as drug addicts. Not a pretty picture, but one that will hopefully force you to examine your "lifestyle choice" with a new perspective.

Whatever glamour that was once associated with cigarette smoking has long since been dispelled. Smoking is not glamorous nor are the various illnesses smoking contributes to glamorous. Health and well-being are glamorous. Vitality is glamorous.

Being active is glamorous.

About 90% of the people who quit smoking experience the same symptoms drug addicts experience when trying to kick their habit,

* Craving for tobacco
* Hunger
* Irritability
* Insomnia

* Headaches
* Coughing
* Anxiety
* Dizziness

If you want to quit smoking, the important thing to remember is that these symptoms are temporary. The long-term health benefits that quitting can bring are not!

There are many books and publications available that are devoted to the problem of kicking the cigarette habit. One of the better ones is *Kick It!* by Judy Perlmutter, founder of Habit Breakers Program. The book can be found at most bookstores.

Exactly what is the cardiac benefit of not smoking?

While it is true that there are real benefits that tobacco lends to the smoker, these benefits are far outweighed by the perils of smoking. Any program designed to prevent heart disease MUST address the issue of smoking. If you can stop smoking you will reduce your risk factor by half. Again, if you can quit permanently, regardless of how long you've smoked, you can reduce your risk of cardiovascular disease to the same risk level as a non-smoker after about two years of abstinence.

Okay, I'm going to get down from my soapbox now. In fact, I'll get down just long enough to let someone else on. Sylvia, a resident of an active adult community for 11 years, lost her husband to a heart attack.

"We were both heavy smokers," she says. "But after John died, I stopped to examine my life. I missed John terribly, but I knew I had to go on—not just for me but for my two daughters and their families."

"I decided definitely to quit when my youngest grandchild, Billy, told me he wouldn't kiss me anymore."

"'Why not?' I asked him, thinking we were playing a silly game. But his answer was anything but silly to me. He said he didn't like the way I smelled because of the cigarettes."

"I decided to quit after John died. But it was Billy who convinced me that the time was now."

"That was three years ago. I won't pretend it was easy, but if what the doctor says is true, Billy did me the best favor he could have done—he convinced me to stop a terrible habit that was terribly bad for me."

"Besides, I couldn't stand going to my daughters' homes and having to go outside to have a cigarette. It was horrible, but they wouldn't allow smoking inside the house. I didn't like it but..."

"Well, I quit. That's the important thing. I got through the hard part and now I feel better. Food tastes better. I have better wind when I walk."

"I feel good."

"I only wish John would have quit too—a long, long time ago."

Chapter Thirty-two
S-E-X.

Healthy and active lives remain the most important goal for mature adults. For most of us, that means that we have to discuss a subject long taboo in our society—Sex and the Active, Mature Adult.

I know that sounds like a bad book or movie, but in fact, it is a reality in our lives.

I have interviewed well over 300 active adults between the ages of 65 and 85 and I asked them all, Do you still enjoy sex? The answers I received were filled with humor and humanity—and honesty.

"If it's a choice between sex and golf, I'd pick golf. It's easier to putt around," one duffer replied.

Another said, "I think I do."

Yet another replied, "In my dreams."

These replies represented the minority of responses, a minority that suggested that sex and sexuality had somehow passed them by. Others replied that they enjoyed sex "very much."

One was very emphatic in her response. "Oh yes!"

Another said, "Too much."

While one woman suggested that she was "a virgin again. I haven't had sex in so long." Another said she was enjoying sex more than ever and that she was enjoying being free from the worry of getting pregnant.

"If my children only knew!" was a familiar refrain from the men and women I spoke with.

One woman laughed then got quiet and then chuckled. "You know, when my children visit, I have to remember to be real quiet," she confided in a whisper.

Some men and women enjoy sexual activity once a week. Some less. Most defined their sexual pleasure more in terms of the quality of their sex lives than the quantity.

"With the right partner, it's wonderful," one woman said.

Another man compared sex to a "log burning slowly," while another said that sex wasn't like an earthquake, "more like a tremor."

Many people engage in sex more during their retirement than they had at any time since their honeymoons.

"I have so much time now."

His wife agreed. "Now we can lounge around

and enjoy being sensual. Before we were always so rushed. Or tired. Between work, the house, the kids... the list goes on and on. But now, we have each other and all the time in the world."

"We're much closer now. Much more intimate."

While many enjoyed sex *more* often in their retirement years, others engaged in sex less. "It's like eating ice cream," one woman said. "You can only have one dip a month."

Regardless of the "amount" of sex, what was clear from everyone's response was that, one way or another, sex and sexuality was still important to them. However, with age has come a certain understanding and honesty.

False modesty and humility often give way to the years. I was in a restaurant not too long ago when a woman at a nearby table took ill and an ambulance was called. When they showed up, they evaluated her and then decided to attach a heart monitor to her. In doing so, they explained that they needed to place pads by her collar bone and on her side, but that they wouldn't expose too much.

"Oh go right ahead," the woman said. "I'm too old to care about silly things anymore."

Indeed, mature adults are more used to the indignities of medical check-ups and evaluations and of the tricks time plays on the body. Not that we necessarily love those tricks. We've just begun to come to terms with them.

So too with our sexuality. No, we are not the same young people we were in our teens and twenties. But what we have lost in strength and stamina we have gained in understanding and gentleness.

One gentleman compared it to tennis. He had his two grandsons, about 13 and 15, visiting him and he was on one side of the net while they were on the other. Although they clearly had the advantage in terms of wind, speed and strength, grandad more than compensated with anticipation, smart play and well-placed shots.

"I don't think so much about sex anymore," he said, concluding his analogy. "I think about making love an awful lot."

Our bodies are not what they were, but those of us who are honest always knew that the best part about sex was our imaginations and, in terms of our imaginations, we've only gotten better!

In many ways, these changes—whether we embrace them or mask them—are truly bittersweet. One woman I spoke with recalled a visit with her college-aged daughter.

"We were walking down the street and a number of male heads turned. As much as I was proud of my daughter's beauty, I was doubly proud of the whistles at me." What's age got to do with it?

Chapter Thirty-three
Changes. Physical. Emotional.

Now that we're ready to enjoy the things of youth, we are no longer young. That is no cause of despair, just to understand and to adapt.

As some of the comments I received regarding sex and sexuality indicate, sex doesn't have to end.

It can get even better.

So much of our sexuality is a function of what we're taught by society and, as those of us a bit younger in years and experience know, much of what we're taught is incorrect. For example, few life changes are as misunderstood and vilified as menopause, that time in a woman's life when menstruation ceases. However, the societal stereotypes suggesting that menopausal women are hard to live with, irrational, exhausted, etc. tend to be misconceptions which, unfortunately for too many, turn into self-fulfilling prophesies.

"Oh sure," said Betty, "I'd heard all the talk about how bitchy I was supposed to get when I went through the change. And I'll tell you the truth, I was concerned."

"I had more anxiety anticipating menopause than I ever had during menopause—or after."

"All the fears... I can almost laugh at them now if they hadn't been so real then... that I would suffer a quick physical decline, that I would get all wrinkled and that I would no longer be feminine or attractive."

Betty has maintained her femininity and her attractiveness with careful attention to diet and exercise. She dresses well and, more than anything, she enjoys a positive outlook.

"I also really understood the things that make another person genuinely attractive to another person—intelligence, humor, empathy."

"When everything was said and done, I believe I became a more attractive person after I retire — —which, for me, also means after menopause.

In my discussion with Betty, I was most impressed by her attitude and her straightforward opinions. So I felt comfortable asking her, "What about sex?"

"Ah sex," she sighed, smiling slightly. "I still enjoy sex. Very much. In many ways more. In other ways less. But it is different now. It is definitely different."

For Betty, sex and sexuality was a slightly different issue because her husband passed away when she was 49, leaving her to contend first with her grief and then with the prospect of dating and renewed sexual feelings.

"It was hard at fist. I dated with some regularity for nearly two years before I met Frank at a seniors' dance. We've been together since and life just keeps getting better."

As we talked more intimately, Betty shared this bit of wisdom— "In my own discussions with women my age I've learned that not much changes after menopause in a real way. That a woman who was sexually active before menopause will be sexually active after menopause. And women with low self-esteem and little satisfaction from life will have the same difficulties gaining self-esteem or satisfaction from life that she had before going through menopause."

What Betty emphasized from her own experience was that the loss of sexuality or sexual desire after menopause was a myth.

Despite the full range of society myth regarding menopause, there are only two physical changes that can be directly attributed to menopause. One is both the result of menopause and the definition of it—changes in the menstrual cycle leading to the permanent cessation of menstruation and hot flashes and sweats (which, though uncomfortable and sometimes embarrassing, generally stop on their own accord after a year or so.

There is disagreement on whether these changes are, in fact, the result of diminished estrogen production and therefore some care should be taken before considering estrogen replacement therapy to address these changes.

Some women never experience these changes to any significant degree. Others are plagued terribly by them.

When she bid good-bye that day, Betty was smiling. She was the picture of health and happiness at 72 years old.

She was off to meet Frank for their afternoon walk along the nature trail. She sighed as she stepped out into the sunshine, smiling even more broadly.

Chapter Thirty-four
You're Changing.
Not Necessarily Depressed.

There is no question that change is hard. Yes, it can be exciting, thrilling, exhilarating—all those wonderful things—but those of us who have lived a lifetime know that whatever else change represents, it represents the need to adapt, to work, to grow. That's often hard.

Even a move to a new house—a wonderful change— is difficult. There are good-byes to people and memories and there is the very difficult physical task of moving.

Life changes are also hard. The changes that come along with retirement are no more or less difficult than any other changes or periods of change in life.

And *that's* the important thing to remember about the transition into the more mature years. It is a change, with difficulties, joys, challenges and problems, but it is like the other life changes you have already undergone—successfully!

Suggestions that menopause leads to serious depression run counter to recent studies which show that there is no greater incidence of depression during the menopausal years than at any other time in life. Indeed, there are many who consider "mid-life crises" to be myths and to have no greater significance than adjustments at any other point in a person's life.

We all have visions of what our lives should be like—and what we want our retirement to be like. Sometimes those visions become reality. Other times, they do not.

For example, Don had looked forward to his retirement because, to him, it meant he would have to take many more fishing trips than he could during his working years. However, his wife, Margaret, put a stop to his plans when she told him that she had no intention of being nothing but a "camp wife and cook."

She wanted them to enjoy their retirement together—not have their retirement be a continuation of the things she liked least about her life before retirement.

By the same token, Karen found that she enjoyed her husband's retirement less than either of them could have anticipated. While she continued to do the things that she was used to doing, Eliot was constantly around the house, "getting in the way."

For Karen, it was like "having another kid. Only worse."

Like any change, retirement—the mature

years—demand adjustments. Couples who are lucky enough to enjoy their mature years together have to really do precisely that—enjoy them *together.* "I never could have anticipated just how wonderful these years would be," Phyllis told me just the other day. "Because Ed always had to work so hard I felt like we never really grew together. I was focused on the kids, he was focused on his career."

"Even after the kids were grown, my own interests were separate from his."

"The adjustment was strange at first. Not difficult, but strange. We suddenly had all this time together and we didn't know what to do with it."

"It was like meeting a new person, a person you'd had a long correspondence with for many years, but you hadn't ever really met."

"We began going to museums. I took up golf because that was something he enjoyed. He attended a couple of evening classes with me at the local college." She smiled here. "He even took a yoga class with me. If you know Ed, you know what a gesture that was."

It was a process of getting to know one another again after a lifetime together that prompted Ed and Phyllis to sell their home and move into a retirement community.

"We just decided that we should enjoy all our time together."

"Not that we don't do things individually," Ed said. "I still like my poker games and billiards. Phyllis still likes having lunch with her lady friends."

"That's what makes being here so perfect. We have a community of people like us, older men and women who still like to do things. When we want to be with others, they're here for us. When we want to be by ourselves, we have that too."

"I tell you, I haven't been this happy since I lived in the dorms as a college student. I couldn't imagine a better way to live."

For adults who plan—and who stay open to new things—the retirement years are a wonderful, fulfilling period of their lives. Sure, there are challenges. Our bodies begin to betray us. Some things are more difficult. Other things are less difficult.

It's a trade-off, one that I think most of us are very happy with.

Chapter Thirty-five
It's Not Just Women Who Change

Although studies of sexual activity indicate that two-thirds of men remain sexually active up to the age of 70. In fact, the best predictor whether or not sexual activity will continue throughout life is a regular expression of sexual activity *throughout* life.

I have heard more than one resident refer to her golden years as the "golden years of sex." She also complained that too many older men and women are not sexually active simply because they believe that they *shouldn't* be more sexually active.

"They've bought into that whole stereotype that us older folks don't or shouldn't enjoy or engage in sexual activity. Hogwash!"

This resident was 73 when she made this statement.

The changes that most women undergo come about in a relatively short period of time, changes in a man's sexuality are gradual, beginning as far back as his early 20s. For men, advancing age brings about very real changes in sexuality

"I enjoyed the closeness more than the actual satisfaction. I don't know if I'm saying that exactly right, but I think you know what I mean," Allan said.

Liz nodded her head and gave her husband's hand a squeeze. "I do," she said.

Like all changes, these changes in sexuality have to be understood and accepted. Some men, when they notice these changes taking place, worry that they spell the end of their sexual ability. Too often, this worry creates a self-fulfilling prophesy.

The greatest obstacle to satisfactory sexuality is the same obstacle many people struggle with in their younger years—fear and ignorance.

There is every indication that, barring illness or psychological blocks, there is no reason that a man shouldn't be able to enjoy sex well into his 80s.

The old saw, "The mind is willing, but the body..." is only partly true. Mature adults have to contend with changes in their bodies, but they also benefit from the wisdom of experience and years.

"I've found that I enjoy sex more and more," one older woman said to me. "However, I think hon est communication between partners is as important in older lovers as younger ones.

I would only add that this woman celebrated her seventieth birthday three weeks ago.

There is so much life and joy in the older years to those who simply reach out to it.

What's Age Got To Do With It?

Chapter Thirty-six
The Active Life Sometimes Means Coping and Growing

Changes. So many changes. While so many are wonderful to accept others require some work. Later life can be a wonderful experience, but we all know that there are many obstacles along the way.

"I thought that when Joe suffered his heart attack that my world would come to an end."

Mary's reaction to her husband's heart attack was understandable. Fortunately, he was in that group of heart attack victims who survived. However, having survived, he had to learn how to cope.

"The doctors assured me that my heart was okay. I was lucky. Damage was minimal and what damage had occurred was in a relatively benign area. Physically, they told me that everything would be fine.

"They showed me how I had to change my diet. Explained that I needed to lose a little weight and to begin an exercise program."

"Getting ready to leave the hospital, I was nothing if not grateful. I wanted nothing more than to get out of that place and get on with my life. But then, I stood up from the wheelchair and walked a few steps to the car. I was shocked. I was exhausted. Winded. I thought the doctors must have been wrong."

Joe was scared to walk from one room to another, fearing that his shortness of breath meant he was going to collapse any moment.

Joe was wrong. His breathlessness when he left the hospital was the result of extended bed rest. His breathlessness at home was the result of fear. His fear, in turn, led to depression. For three months, Joe suffered with the certainty that even if he didn't die, he would never have a "normal" life again.

All this was relayed to me as I walked—at a brisk pace—with Joe and Mary along the nature trail. Keeping up with them was not an easy task.

"So what changed for you?" I asked him.

"Well a lot of the change came about naturally. I mean if you spend day after day expecting to die and then you keep not dying, well, that makes an impression. Then, Mary finally put her foot down and insisted that I talk to someone. That helped a lot."

"I just couldn't bear to see him suffering anymore. And, honestly, he was making it hard for me as well. It reached a point where I was scared to leave the house because I didn't know what would happen to him."

With counseling, Joe reached a better understanding of what had happened to him and, more to the point, what he could and could not do.

"I believed that I had to avoid any kind of excitement. I missed the NBA play-offs because I was worried I'd get too caught up in the game. I wouldn't drive during rush hour for the same reason. I avoided family discussions."

"Personally, I think missing the basketball game was more stress than if he had watched it," Mary noted.

Joe grinned. "Maybe. The point was, I avoided all that. And I needn't have. I am much happier being involved."

Joe also explained how much happier he was being physically active. "I don't know that I'm going to run a marathon, but I sure enjoy these walks. In fact, I've reached a point where I do just about everything I did before my attack."

"I built up gradually and I checked in with my doctor, but over some time, I was able to get back to where I was."

Exercise is a vital component in everyone's life—whether they have suffered a heart attack or not.

"It took Joe a while to get back on track," Mary said, looking at Joe and smiling. "And me too. That heart attack threw us both for a loop. But we got through it and we're better off now than we've been for a long, long time."

Joe nodded his head. When I left the two of them they were continuing their brisk walk. Their conversation wandered to what they were going to do for dinner that evening. The last I heard was a plan to share a meal with their neighbors, the Millers.

Chapter Thirty-seven
Did You See My Parents?

I am looking high and low

Did you see my parents?

It used to be they were always home

Dad on the couch watching TV

Mom in the kitchen cooking or cleaning.

What happened to my parents?

The house they lived in for 40 years, now has been sold. They left a note ("We are out of here—no more maintenance, no more snow removal, no more grass cutting—we are off to a new Lifestyle.")
I called my mom to ask her what she made for dinner, and she replies "reservations."

Dad just bought a new BMW Convertible. My friends say they see him riding around town playing Glory Days on his new CD player.

Where are my parents?

Mom and Dad work out at the gym three or four times a week. What happened? They always used to baby-sit!!!

I called my parents, and would you believe it I got an answering machine that said— "Sorry Mom and Dad are not here right now because we have Tennis Lessons at 8:00am, Bridge at 10:00am, Lunch with the Morgans at 12:00, Jazzercise at 2:00pm, Line dancing at 4:00pm, Dinner with the McDonalds at 6:00pm, Movies at 7:30pm.

Love ya, Mom and Dad."

What happened to my parents?

Chapter Thirty-eight
To My Husband

My ability to appreciate, to understand and to love the many, many mature adults that I have met over the past decade has been made so much easier and pleasurable by the constant love and support of my own husband. And so, remaining true to my claim that love and life continue on, I would like to conclude with this " song " to my husband—

Feelings of Yesterday

I would like to thank you, darling
For all the years we've been together.

For all the times, good and bad
For sharing life's secrets with me.

I would like to thank you, darling,
for the miracle of our children,
the memories of yesterdays gone by,
Christmas trees and Easter bunnies.

I would like to thank you, darling,
For being there in troubles, pain and sorrow

You have given me a treasure of life
locked in my heart of yesterday
forever.

You've been the one to take me through,
to show me how.

You've been my rock,
my knight in armor.

You've been the glow around my world.

You have given me a life of contentment.

Looking back, I can't complain.
You are the one and only man I've ever loved.

You are my dreams of yesterday.
You will be my dreams of tomorrow.

I love you more and more each day, so

I just want to thank you, darling
For being my best friend
and for sharing your life with me.

Chapter Thirty-nine
Adult Communities

So you think retirement would be boring: You ask, " What is it really like to retire today in the 'nineties' in an active adult community?"

The answer is easy:

It's getting up in the morning looking forward to a busy day. The first thing you will have to do is check the calendar of events. If you are smart it will be on your refrigerator. You do not want to miss out on any activities. There will be so many choices, you will have to find the ones that suit you. There is a new breed of active adults retiring today, you'll love being with them sharing happy new memories.

It's never feeling alone.
It's having the freedom to do the things you never had time to do before.
It's thinking young.
It's keeping fit, eating health.
It's having the feeling of excitement again, like going to your first prom. That's how you feel about your new lifestyle.
It's smiles on everyone's faces.
It's participating in activities and events you never thought you could do before.
It's feeling good about life again.

Chapter Forty
Ever Consider an Adult Community?

While all mature adults face some of the health concerns that I've mentioned in the preceding chapters, those who consider a retirement community will find a community of people who not only understand those concerns, but are determined to overcome obstacles and live life as fully and enjoyably as possible.

Some potential residents are always sure to express their fear that selling the home they've lived in for so many years.

"I just know if I sold my home now I would be sorry," one woman said. "Twenty-five years of memories. My children were born here. They grew up here."

"Hasn't anyone ever felt that way about their home before?" I was glad I was able to answer that question. I told her, "Of course, most people. We all love our memories. They are precious to us—and they should be. I think if you were to ask most of the residents here they would tell you that they feared they would miss their homes too. But I think they will all tell you that they're glad they moved."

The woman looked at me as if she thought I was exaggerating the case, so I invited her to pick anyone she saw and ask them about their feelings. She pointed to Sam, a five-year resident.

I walked her over to where Sam was talking to another resident, Jim. "Sam, I know you moved here a few years ago, you sold the house you lived in for 30 years. Was that difficult?"

"Of course it was," Sam said. "And there was so much stuff..."

"I don't mean like that," I said. "Was it difficult emotionally?"

"Not as much as I thought it would be," he said. "I was reluctant at first. I held out much longer than my wife. She was tired of the cleaning. She said we didn't need all that room anymore."

"I think it was the last big snowfall when I had to shovel the snow out of the driveway that I was finally decided."

"I did miss the old house—for about two months. Then I found myself kicking myself, wishing I had made the move ten years earlier."

"You can't beat this place. It's beautiful. There's great people around. I don't have to shovel snow. And there's so many interesting and fun things to do here."

"Sam's right," Jim piped in. "A house is just a house. It's the people who make it. I wouldn't trade this bunch in for anything."

As we walked away, my prospective resident whispered to me with a smile, "You sure they weren't rehearsed?"

I laughed. "Pick anyone else," I said, waving my arm at the large number of people enjoying the lovely afternoon. "The answer will be essentially the same."

"I was interested in Sam's comment about the snow," she said. "That's one thing my husband would be very glad to leave behind—maintenance and gardening." She glanced around at the beautifully manicured flower beds and lawns. "Who takes care of all that here?"

"It's taken care of by the maintenance crew—and it's all included in your maintenance agreement. Your only responsibility here is to enjoy your new lifestyle."

"That sounds wonderful," she agreed. "One of the things that I like best about having the house is when my friends or relatives come to visit I feel that I can be free with my hospitality. Would I feel the same way here?"

"I certainly hope so. Your family and friends are welcome to use the facilities here. Most of the communities give their guests badges to wear while visiting, allowing them to enjoy the community."

"My daughter is going to be graduating college in another two years. I have been looking forward to having a party for her at the house. If I lived here, would I still be able to give her a private party at the clubhouse?"

"Absolutely," I replied. "The process is really very simple—and no different from booking any other facility. You would book your party into the Calendar of Events with the Concierge or Director of Activities. Each community has its own specific rules, but the Concierge or Director of Activities will help you from soup to nuts."

Chapter Forty-one
Are You Ready for a Change

So you think retirement would be boring: You wonder what it would be like to be retired in the 1990's. Wonder no more!

Living an active adult life is getting up in the morning and looking forward to a busy day. It's going to to your refrigerator door to check out the Calendar of Events so you don't miss out on anything.

There's a new breed of active adults retiring today. You'll love being with them and sharing happy new memories. Retirement today means:

* never feeling alone
* having the freedom to do things you never had time for before
* being on constant vacation
* thinking young
* keeping fit, eating healthy
* having the feeling of excitement again. Like going to your first prom

"Well, I guess that I'm ready for a change."

"But what can an active adult community offer me?" my friend asked.

I raised my eyebrows. "Oh, just a handful of

things," I said, half-joking. "Let me give you a list."

* Brisk walking club along the three mile trail
* Aqua-aerobics classes
* State of the art health and fitness facilities complete with latest exercise equipment men's and ladies' locker rooms
* Saunas
* Billiards
* Computer facility
* Card rooms—men's and ladies'
* Library
* Great room with big-screen television for special events and movies
* Stained glass classes
* Social dances
* Wood carving
* Camera club
* Design your own t-shirt activities
* Plant club
* Flower arrangement classes
* Line dancing classes—country, ballroom, etc.
* Ceramics
* Cooking clubs—Mexican, Italian, Vegetarian, Healthy, etc.
* Cocktail hour (4-6) in the clubhouse
* Juice bar
* Travel club
* Day trips, Atlantic City, etc.
* Massage specialist
* Fishing trips
* Indoor-outdoor swimming pool w/instructor
* Tennis courts, lighted, w/instructor
* Shuffleboard—for fun and tournaments
* Boccie—for fun and tournaments

* Horseshoes—regular contests
* "Kick the Can"
* Men's and Ladies' softball
* Girls' club
* Men's club
* Drama club
* Book discussion group
* Superbowl party
* Game night—chess, checkers, backgammon, etc.
* Rent the Great Room for parties
* Woodlock Pines Park
* The three Little bakers
* Hunterdon Play House
* Papermill Millburn—day trips
* Reports
* Villa Roma
* Restaurants
    - Water's Edge, Bayville
    - Old Mill Inn
    - Doolons
    - Castle—Lakewood - Lunch

Busses available
- Classic Bus
- Trollie Tours
- Van Norwick
- Leisure Line

* Jogging club
* Biking club
* Jacuzzi
* Singles club
* Lapidary
* Sewing group
* Painting—oil, chalk, etc.
* Fashion shows
* Bowling

* Roller skating
* Ice skating
* Financial club

When I was finished with the list, I looked at Evelyn. "So, do you think you'd be able to find something to do in an active adult community?"

She laughed. "My Lord, it sounds as if I'd have too much to do."

I shook my head. "You can never have too much available for you to do."

"But I'm exhausted just listening to the list!"

I laughed. "I didn't say you had to do everything, Evelyn. You pick and choose. It's there for you. You don't have to go on trips, but it's nice to know that the trips are available. You can learn tennis, play tennis, meet at the clubhouse, whatever strikes your fancy."

"What I would emphasize is that there is *so much* for you to do. If you've never played Boccie before—or horseshoes—try it! You might find it to be the very activity you come to love."

"Maybe you've never had the time, or had the instruction, to learn how to create stained glass windows or do wood carving. Now you do. Ceramics is a favorite with many of the people I work with. They send their vases and artwork to their children just as proudly as they once displayed their children's artwork."

"Or, maybe you want to play in the billiards tournament. Wouldn't that be fun? Wouldn't your children be shocked to see a billiards trophy in your living room?"

"Or maybe you want to join the computer club or learn to cook healthy meals. Maybe the stock market has always been a mystery to you. If so, join the Financial club."

"Personally, I think you would love line dancing or trim-a-cize."

Evelyn was chuckling softly, overwhelmed by the picture I was painting for her.

"I just don't understand why you or anyone would want to stay home in a big house with all its responsibilities when you could be enjoying all the benefits of an active adult community."

She shrugged her shoulders. "I must say, you make a compelling argument."

"I'll tell you what, you come and visit me at work and I'll take you on a tour. Then you decide what you think. Fair enough?"

She nodded her head.

I didn't have a doubt in my mind that she would become a wonderful member of an adult community. She was ready and I knew her husband was.

As much as I proclaim the benefits of the active adult lifestyle, even in an adult community, it is still up to the individual to take advantage of all the wonderful opportunities available. It opens doors to single adults too. You don't have to be afraid to live alone. The security is great! Just a phone call away.

But will I like it??? I've asked residents who have moved in to come back in three months and tell me what their thoughts are of their new lifestyle. I already know what they are going to say, because it's said to me over and over again. "I should have done this years ago"; "I feel younger"; "I'm so happy." I feel most people are shocked when they finally do it and retire, and learn what a wonderful life it really is!

Listed below are some of the quotes from active adults about retirement today:

"I love retirement. I have so many new friends to do things with."

"I thought I was too young, but since the first day I moved in, I've loved it. You never get lonely."

"To us, this is the Fountain of Youth! Stick around and grow younger and younger. We love it."

"It's like being a kid in a candy store surrounded by all the things you ever wanted!"

"When we go on vacation, we can't wait to come back home."

"We're having a ball. We need another day in the week to do all we'd like to do."

"Until we moved, we never needed a calendar. Wish we could tell the whole world, so they could be as happy as we are!" "I think the security is great! I like all the activities." "We love our new exciting lifestyle."

But there are also many, many joys and pleasures. Intimacy, romance, travel, friendship—these are all open to you. Being in a community of like-minded adults, interested and interesting people who enjoy being *active* makes the golden years even more golden.

It's having the best lifestyle.

It's enjoying life to the fullest.

It's putting your head down on your pillow at night exhausted from all the activities and sleeping like a baby.

You can't wait for the next day, because you have another full day of fun and activities going on again.

You have to listen to your tape recorder to receive messages while you are out... again.

It's having to make decisions about going to Atlantic City for the day, or going to Wildwood with 48 other couples for a week.

Perhaps you want to see the Fashion Show sponsored at one of the Clubs, or you may have to go to organ or band practice.

Perhaps you made arrangements to go to lunch with the "Lunch Bunch," which I might add are all men.

The list is endless.

Retiring in the "nineties" is the time to chase butterflies again.

Chapter Forty-two
You Are Ready for a Retirement Community, If You...

...are 55 or older

...are bored

...owned a big house and the children are gone

...are tired of maintenance

...hate cutting grass

...hate shoveling snow

...like to travel

...like to have fun

...have an attitude???

...are ready for a change

...would like the feeling of being on a continuous vacation

... are now ready for the fun stage of life

—Want More Information about Seminars?—

There are many other questions about changing lifestyles that Ms. Zarrilli is frequently asked by people over 55, such as " How do you make new friends at 'our age?'" — "Are there new rules for dating?" — "How can I stay close to my kids and grandkids after I retire?"

Her answers often confirm that these concerns are normal and a big part of the process of making a change. However, she can also offer reassurances that the other part of this change is a much happier and healthier lifestyle.

Active adults with specific questions about pre-retirement and retirement lifestyles are welcome to contact Ms. Zarrilli at:

Ms. Shirley Zarrilli
13 Tilton Road
Bricktown, NJ 08723

(Please enclose a self-addressed—stamped envelope and a processing fee of 5.00 with your letter.)

WHAT'S AGE GOT TO DO WITH IT?

A CELEBRATION OF LIFE

SECOND EDITION

2000/184 PAGES/PERFECT/ISBN 0-7872-6776-7

ORDER FORM ORDER FORM ORDER FORM

QTY	VOLUME DISCOUNTS	PRICE* (PER COPY)	TOTAL
	1-10 COPIES	$17.00	
	11-50 COPIES—25% DISCOUNT	$12.75	
	51+ COPIES—40% DISCOUNT	$10.20	
	AL, AZ, CA, CO, FL, GA, IA, IL, IN, KS, KY, LA, MA, MD, MI, MN, NC, NJ, NM, NY, OH, PA, TN, TX, VA, WA, & WI add sales tax		
	Add shipping: order total $17-25 = $4; $26-50 = $5; $51-75 = $6; $76-100 = $7; $101-150 = $8; $151- or more = $9		
	TOTAL		

*Prices are subject to change without notice.

❒ Check enclosed, payable to Kendall/Hunt Publishing Company

❒ Charge my credit card upon shipment:

❒ American Express ❒ MasterCard ❒ VISA

Credit Card No. ______________________

Exp. Date ______________________

Signature ______________________

Name ______________________

Address ______________________

City ______________________

State ______________________

ZIP+ 4/Postal Code ______________________

Phone (   ) ______________________

KENDALL / HUNT
PUBLISHING COMPANY
4050 Westmark Drive P.O. Box 1840
Dubuque Iowa 52004-1840